GOD HUNTING

A diary of spiritual discovery

Copyright © Scripture Union 2011
First published 2011; reprinted 2013
ISBN 978 1 84427 533 5

Scripture quotations are taken from the HOLY BIBLE, TODAY'S NEW INTERNATIONAL
VERSION, (TNIV) © 2004 by International Bible Society. Used by permission of Hodder
& Stoughton, a division of Hodder Headline Ltd. All rights reserved.

The right of Jo Swinney to be identified as author of this work has been asserted by her
in accordance with the Copyright, Designs and Patents Act 1988.
British Library Cataloguing-in-Publication Data: a catalogue record of this book
is available from the British Library.

Cover design and internal layout by Martin Lore www.martinlore.co.uk
Printed and bound in India by Thomson Press India Ltd

Scripture Union is an international Christian charity working with churches in more
than 130 countries.

Thank you for purchasing this book. Any profits from this book support SU in England and
Wales to bring the good news of Jesus Christ to children, young people and families and
to enable them to meet God through the Bible and prayer.

Find out more about our work and how you can get involved at:

www.scriptureunion.org.uk (England and Wales)
www.suscotland.org.uk
www.suni.co.uk
www.scriptureunion.org (USA)
www.su.org.au (Australia)

For Ally and Alice

Acknowledgements

The writing of this book has left me with a heavy debt of gratitude and a thank you in print is poor repayment, but it comes very sincerely from me to all of you who have helped in your various ways.

Thank you to everyone who bought me precious writing time by looking after my girls, especially Barbara, Julia, Rachael, Hedy, the Eastwoods, the Styles, Camilla, Alex and Ashleigh. I can say perfectly truthfully that I couldn't have done it without you!

Thank you to the people whose stories and wisdom have enriched the content in this volume, particularly Pete, Joanna, Chris, Christoph, Libby and Fiona.

The content was also vastly improved by my mother, Miranda, who read and commented on early drafts and kept me going with vast quantities of encouragement. Kate Power also cast her eagle eye over the manuscript – faithful are the wounds of a friend! I am very blessed to have such people in my life and involved in my writing. Thank you both.

Thank you to all the people I have worked with on this project at Scripture Union. 'Tricia Williams has been a gentle, understanding and encouraging editor, who I've enjoyed working with greatly.

Thank you Shawn, Alexa and Charis for being my safe place and for keeping me humble, amused and challenged. You are the most amazing family, and I am so incredibly grateful for each of you.

I am dedicating this book to my friends Ally and Alice. We prayed together on a weekly basis for four years, and I can't say strongly enough how important these times were. Thank you both for your company on this journey, for your godliness, wisdom and honesty. You are seekers after God, and you have inspired me more than you will know.

Jo Swinney
Chalfont St Peter
June 2010

Contents

Visit www.scriptureunion.org.uk/godhunting or www.joswinney.com to hear podcasts of the interviews featured in *God Hunting*.

About the author…

Jo has a masters in Christian Studies from Regent College, Vancouver. She is the author of *Through the Dark Woods* and *Cheerful Madness*, and is a regular contributor to several magazines. She lives with her husband Shawn and two small daughters in South Buckinghamshire, and is online at www.joswinney.com.

'COME NEAR TO GOD...'

Come near to God and he will come near to you. Wash your hands, you sinners, and purify your hearts, you double-minded. Grieve, mourn and wail. Change your laughter to mourning and your joy to gloom. Humble yourselves before the Lord, and he will lift you up.

JAMES 4:8–10

To do: Find God

Some write them on their hands. Some dictate them to their assistants. Some jot them on their BlackBerry, cram them onto old receipts, or keep them looping around their minds as they go about their day. Some swear by them, others deny they have the need for them, but in truth we are all slaves to our lists. And I will be the first to stand up and admit it.

I am a busy person like everyone else. I have multiple lists on the go at any one time, from shopping lists, to people commitments, to long-term goals, and my planner is pleasingly hectic-looking. I have a feisty preschooler, a second baby on the way, and an emotionally-needy cat. My husband, Shawn, is a full-time youth pastor in the process of becoming ordained in the Anglican Church. Our home sees scores of people flow through its doors each week, and I struggle to keep on top of even basic domestic tasks – my welcome is always followed closely by an apology for the state of the house. I am a writer, and occasional speaker, and this is the official work component of my life. I am also on the committee of a local toddler group, run a teenage girls' monthly get-together, and lead an Alpha group. I try to keep in touch with family and friends, feed my mind with good books and my family with good food, and stay on top of the piles of paperwork that seem to be a prerequisite of adulthood. Before I got pregnant I went running three times a week and attended Weight Watchers – those activities have dropped out of my schedule temporarily, so I suppose I have gained some extra time along with the baby weight.

That is my busyness. I am sure yours is much more impressive. Maybe, like me, in surveying your life you feel a combination of pride and shame at the bulging contents of each day: pride, because we are conditioned to value ourselves by our productivity; shame, because we know that moving at such a speed is inevitably detrimental to our spiritual, emotional and physical health.

I am not actually anti-busyness *per se*, and neither is the Bible. The book of Proverbs warns that lazy people won't get to eat venison (12:27), that they make for disastrous employees ('vinegar to the teeth and smoke to the eyes', 10:26), they get hungry because they can't be bothered to lift their forks from the plate to their mouths (19:24) and they use ridiculous excuses not to leave the house, which would be far too exerting ('There's a lion outside! I'll be killed in the public square!' 22:13). Working hard and filling your days is not a bad thing. God gave Adam and Eve a demanding job in the Garden of Eden, and ever since then there has been work to do on six out of every seven days. But it becomes a bad thing when we use it as an excuse for a neglected relationship with God.

There is a danger that we allow the things we do to define us, to give us our purpose, meaning and identity. Sometimes our activities shape us, rather than the other way round. The apostle Paul at one point lived by this principle. He had a very impressive list of credentials, recounted for us, somewhat wryly, in his letter to the Philippians: 'Circumcised on the eighth day, of the people of Israel, of the tribe of Benjamin, a Hebrew of Hebrews; in regard to the law, a Pharisee; as for zeal, persecuting the church; as for righteousness based on the law, faultless' (Philippians 3:5,6). But he comes to consider all these excellent attributes and accomplishments totally worthless compared to knowing Christ Jesus. What he strives towards is to know God, to become like him, to participate in his sufferings (verse 10), and to end up in heaven (verse 14). How does he strive? He says, 'I press on towards the goal to win the prize for which God has called me heavenwards' (verse 14) but what does his pressing on actually look like? I'm not sure, but I do know it sounds like an effort. There is nothing passive about Paul's spiritual life. There should be nothing passive about ours.

Gordon MacDonald, in his book *Ordering Your Private World*, draws the distinction between being driven and being called. He says that, 'Called people have strength from within, perseverance and power that are impervious to the blows from without.'[1] Who we are and what we do are not the same thing, but the distinction gets lost when we don't invest in our spiritual lives. Here is how that might work out in practice for me: if I am secure in my place in God's family, I won't crash and burn if I don't get the next publishing contract. If I am convinced of God's love for me, it won't hurt quite so badly if I get a bad review or a letter from an offended reader. If my mind is saturated in biblical truth, I won't accept anyone else's version of my worth. I want to be honest with you in these pages, so I must confess that I am a very long way from that level of sanity and security. But I long to get there. I long for intimacy with God that keeps me safe from things that don't matter, to go about my day in the company of the Trinity, to fall asleep in conversation with Jesus and to have crazy Spirit-filled dreams until I wake the next day. I want to give my busyness and exhaustion to God, see what he will do with it and through it, and discover what life lived to the full really looks like.

Maybe you can relate to that desire. Maybe, like me, you long for spiritual depth. You would love to have a connection to God that moors you in choppy waters. You are afraid that your house is built on sand and not on rock, and you want to dig better foundations before a storm tests your craftsmanship. Is it possible to do this without withdrawing to a mountain cave with a Bible, a blanket and a can of baked beans?

Busyness is a disease of our times in Western culture, and busyness is the excuse that many of us give when we admit to the poverty of our Christian lives. We know the value of the spiritual disciplines such as prayer, Bible study, fasting and solitude, but assume we are too busy to implement them in our daily routines. Holy people with time on their hands are mastering the techniques with dedication and probably even enjoying it at this very moment, as we sit here reading. But it is just unrealistic to hope that the rest of us can incorporate them into life as it is. Or is it?

Meaningful mess

For most of us, God's calling on our lives doesn't involve a retreat to the cloisters of a religious order. There are moments when that might seem appealing, when you are fighting traffic on the way home from a long day at work, when you notice your toddler torturing the baby and are too tired to intervene even though the screaming is giving you a migraine, and when your mobile and your land line are ringing at the same time, and you can't get to them because you are trying to sort out a fast-moving virus on your laptop. At such times you might wistfully imagine the cool of the ancient stones beneath your feet, the soft candlelight flickering gently around the altar and the strains of a soaring descant at evensong. Bliss. Except for the poverty, chastity and obedience bit, which could put a dampener on the ecstasy…

The real challenge is not to give our lives a drastic prune, but to make sure, continuing on in the horticultural vein, that we are branches coming from the vine that is God. Jesus said, 'I am the vine; you are the branches. If you remain in me and I in you, you will bear much fruit; apart from me you can do nothing' (John 15:5). So how does the image translate to reality? How can I really remain in God? What does it mean, and how can I do it?

The means to the end

I think I can do it by forming habits that will draw me closer to God. I cannot expect to feel connected to him if I don't invest in our relationship. This is just good common sense. In *Too Busy Not to Pray* Bill Hybels writes: 'God has invited us to come into his presence. He has told us that he is with us and within us, that he is waiting to hear from us, and that he can and will respond to us. What is more, he has told us what kind of habits we must develop in order to make the most of his blessings.'[2]

Here we come to the tricky issue of time: where is it hiding? Is there any to spare for this all-important task of spiritual growth? Yes – there is always time: we make time for the things we consider important. Somehow they just fit in. Let me give you an example. When I was pregnant with Alexa, I ate as though in training for the Eating Olympics, and the law of cause and effect still being in good working order, I gained a substantial amount of weight. The weight hung around long enough that it ceased to be classifiable as baby weight, and became plain old weight. When it really started to bother me, I found time to attend a weight-loss club on a weekly basis. Who knew that time was there? My grandfather used to remind me frequently of Parkinson's Law: 'Work expands so as to fill the time available for its completion.' The flip side of that law is that it will also contract if there is less time for it. So let's endeavour to skim some precious minutes from wherever we can get it, and hope that everything shakes down to fill what remains.

My neighbours are practising Hindus. In their very small house live two parents, three children and an uncle. Space is at a premium and yet a whole room of this cramped space is devoted to a shrine to their gods. If something is important to us, we make it work, whatever sacrifices to our comfort are involved.

There can be nothing more important than our relationship with God. If we forget this, if we allow the busyness to distract us from our ultimate purpose, quite simply we will not get the prize that Paul was talking about in his letter. Dallas Willard, in *The Great Omission*, contends that: 'The greatest issue facing the world today, with all its heart-breaking needs, is whether those who, by profession or culture, are identified as "Christians" will become disciples – students, apprentices, practitioners – of Jesus Christ, steadily learning from him how to live the life of the Kingdom of the Heavens into every corner of human existence.'[3] Stop right here for a second. This is the point at which we need to determine if we are going to make this a priority. We need only have the seed of the desire to grow – the more we know him the more we will want to know him – but the seed does need to be there.

Back when Jesus was walking around Israel, getting close to him was physically possible. A whole bunch of people literally followed him around the place, listening to his stories, asking him for help with health problems, watching how he dealt with his relationships and trying to understand his teaching. It is a bit harder to get close to a person who is temporarily invisible. But, I hasten to add, entirely possible. And here we get to the concept of 'spiritual disciplines'. This is what we do instead of wearing out our sandal leather walking the dusty roads of first-century Palestine. We pray, we read and absorb the Word of God, the Bible, we get together and worship, we find pockets of silence for meditating and listening to the Holy Spirit, and we weave all we are learning into the fabric of our lives so that knowledge becomes reality. Spiritual disciplines are practices that enable us to deepen our relationship with Christ.

The Experiment

I have shared with you my longing to stop paddling on the shore and wade into deep waters until I am out of my depth. It is time I stopped talking about it and did something. So here is my plan:

I have set myself a challenge. I am going to trial one spiritual discipline per month, until I have worked my way through six of them: prayer, fasting, Bible study, worship, solitude and simplicity. You will be able to see from my experiment if it is worthwhile, or even possible, to invest in your relationship with God through spiritual disciplines in the midst of a crazy schedule. As I practice each discipline I will talk to others about their experiences of this discipline and do some reading. I will share with you any insights I gain. I want to know how these disciplines will impact my relationship with God and by extension, the way I live my life. I want to know what is easy and what is hard about putting them into practice. I want to discover whether they are compatible with my life as it is or whether I need to make big changes to accommodate them.

This is how it will work: each month, I will begin with an appraisal of how the discipline has featured in my life thus far. I will then set out specific goals, such as one twenty-four-hour food fast per week for the fasting month. I will carry a notebook with me at all times and record any thoughts or insights that occur to me, and I will tell you when I fail. I promise to humbly confess to the trials as well as the triumphs, which I hope will encourage you. At the end of the month I will assess the experience – how it felt, what I learned, how easy it was to incorporate into my life, and what it has done to my overall spiritual health.

You can either do it alongside me, or wait until I've finished and make full use of the mistakes I made to make sure you do a better job. You could adopt my goals or tailor-make your own. You might do six months, six weeks or six days. You could do it alone, with a small group or with your family. Or you can read about my experiences, laugh at my expense, give the book to a charity shop and continue on as before. Personally, I think that would be a shame.

Believing in giants is dangerous

Before we set out, I want to ask you something, and I want you to answer honestly. Do you believe in giants? Do you think, in your heart of hearts, that there are people out there who really have it sussed – the kind of people who usually write the books on spiritual matters – and that they tower above you at a height you will never attain? I think most of us live in the shadows of this lofty lot, feeling ashamed and inadequate about our own spiritual stature, and because of this, demotivated and immobilised. Shall we agree to be real, with ourselves and with our fellow journeyers on The Way? We all, as the archetypal school report puts it, 'could do better'. Personally, I am half-hearted, deceitful and lazy when it comes to following Jesus. But we are not going to move forward very fast propelled by shame and trying to hide behind a veneer of false holiness. I will tell you now that when I read Richard Foster I feel intimidated and awed. BUT, we all have our own stories with God, and the task is to know him in our own lives and circumstances, whatever they may be.

Onward

This is an exciting adventure, and terrifying at the same time, because if we search for God, he will be found by us, and then there's no knowing what might happen. As Moses said to the Israelites all those centuries back, 'If... you seek the Lord your God, you will find him if you seek him with all your heart and with all your soul' (Deuteronomy 4:29). Let's go hunting.

CHAPTER ONE

PRAYER

*The four living creatures and the twenty-four elders
fell down before the Lamb. Each one had a harp
and they were holding golden bowls full of incense,
which are the prayers of God's people.*

REVELATION 5:8

Ready, Steady, Procrastinate, Go

Jesus was known to withdraw to quiet places for prayer. I have
withdrawn to a squishy leather sofa in the corner of the Greyhound Pub,
which at nine-thirty in the morning is still not particularly quiet; a large
television is giving me news and sports updates and a couple of rowdy
regulars are getting a head start at the bar. But I have a hot chocolate
at my elbow, a huge pile of books about prayer waiting to be mined for
spiritual treasure, and I am here to pray.

The writer Annie Dillard says that we ought to wear crash helmets to
church,[1] the implication being that meeting with God is a dangerous
business. As I enter this season of prayerfulness, I feel a certain sense
of trepidation. If I am to take prayer seriously, I must face the fact that
I might get burnt by the holiness of God. He might want to talk back to
me. He might want me to take some inconvenient steps of change. My
life might get entirely disrupted.

I think I am OK with this. My basic philosophy is that ultimate meaning and purpose and joy are found in a person's relationship with God. To take this relationship to a new level of intimacy can only be a good thing therefore, but I confess here and now, it is a frightening prospect as well as an exciting one.

I have been praying from babyhood, but a lifetime's practice has not made me particularly proficient. While there have been times when I have found prayer a natural and enjoyable thing to do, there have been long stretches when it has seemed unfeasibly difficult, disappointing and dull. I may be unusual in my frankness about it, but I would be surprised if I was alone in feeling it. My guess is that we all would like to pray more than we do.

At the moment, I mostly pray in a spur of the moment fashion, while out and about and on the move. A couple of times a week I manage to sit down and pray more formally for ten minutes or so, perhaps writing a bit in my journal. Every Wednesday afternoon I meet to pray with two friends, Ally and Alice. All of us have pre-schoolers in tow, which as you can imagine makes the situation a little chaotic. But despite bust-ups over toys, nappy changes and requests for juice, we still manage a smattering of meaningful conversation with each other and with God. I find it much easier to pray with others than by myself, even when there are children crawling over every surface. Each evening I pray with Alexa at bedtime, and often I find that at some point during the day there is a snatched prayer said with a friend or with my husband Shawn.

I have thought a lot about why I find prayer difficult. Here are some of the main reasons:

- I can't see God. When you are talking to someone invisible you can feel a bit like you are talking to yourself.
- I wonder if I am praying to the right person or if my understanding of

the Trinity is so limited that I am addressing a being that doesn't even exist.

- When I am praying alone, I soon feel drained and lose concentration.
- I am not sure how to pray for suffering people and difficult situations, because I don't want to get my hopes up that something might change and risk being disappointed when it doesn't.
- I don't have many quiet spaces in my life and when I do have them I fill them up, and they are not usually filled up with prayer.
- When I begin to pray, I get overwhelmed by how much there is to pray about and I don't know where to begin. Where I really want to begin is with my own little life and its troubles, but that seems self-centred. So I give up before I even start.
- I know this sounds funny, but I feel awkward using regular language to talk to God, because it seems disrespectful. I know that he formed us and doesn't have a problem with us being human and him being divine, but still, I can't help but feel there should be a special way to talk to him.

Perhaps prayer doesn't need to be so hard. One of the things that I am really hoping will happen as a result of this month of prayer is that I can learn to relax a little. I'd like to stop worrying about getting it right, and just do it, in the same unconscious way that I breathe or walk or sleep. I have been reading a book from the seventeenth century called *Experiencing the Depths of Jesus Christ* by Madame Guyon. She writes this:

'I realise that some of you may feel that you are very slow, that you have a poor understanding, and that you are very unspiritual. Dear reader, there is nothing in this universe that is easier to obtain than the enjoyment of Jesus Christ! Your Lord is more present to you than you are to yourself! Furthermore, his desire to give of himself to you is greater than your desire to lay hold of him.'[2]

When the disciples asked Jesus how to pray he didn't say, 'What a stupid question. If you were really holy it would come naturally to you. I am very disappointed that you asked me that.' Instead he gave them a prayer that someone kindly recorded. 'The Lord's Prayer', as it is known, has been helping us communicate with God ever since. Prayer is something we can learn to do better. It is something that we need to be doing if we want to be in a growing relationship with God. And maybe it *should* be as easy as Madame Guyon suggests, because after all we are talking to 'our Father' who loves us and is all ears.

Enough talking. Enough reading. Let's pray.

Week One

I thought I'd start with trying out meditation, until I came upon a warning from Richard Foster in his book, *Prayer*,[3] that this is not for the novice, rather for those who are in a good state of spiritual fitness, and I felt a bit chastened! I flicked quickly to the chapter on simple prayer, which anyone can do. The idea of simple prayer is that you talk unreservedly to God as a child to a father, however mixed your motives, however selfish your requests, and however trivial your concerns. God, Foster assures us, delights in our company, and can work with us whatever state we're in. Thus encouraged, I decided on the following goals for my first week of prayer:

1. **To pray simply**: telling God my immediate concerns without worrying too much about how trite or self-centred they might be.
2. To follow Jeanne Guyon's instructions on '**beholding the Lord**'. Essentially this means entering the presence of God by faith and keeping your mind focused on staying there, refusing to be distracted by other thoughts.
3. Each night before sleep to review the day by asking two questions: 'For what moment today am I most grateful?' And 'For what

moment today am I least grateful?' This is a practice called **'The Examen'**.

Simple prayers

It turned out that my concerns were pretty trivial this week. I seemed to pray a lot about potty training and tantrums, and I have to say it helped to be able to share my frustrations with the Almighty. Whether as a result of my prayers or my daughter's natural abilities in the realms of bowel and temper control, we have seen vast improvements over the last few days – fewer accidents and fewer emotional meltdowns: glory be to God!

Simple prayer fits well into a busy life. It is possible to carry out a conversation with God, albeit frequently interrupted, throughout each frenetic day. I felt a certain freedom in knowing that I didn't have to worry about polishing up the content of my prayers, and I enjoyed the companionship of the ongoing communication. Ania, a Polish psychologist in her early thirties, is a great believer in this kind of prayer:

'Sometimes I pray whilst doing other things, which I find very refreshing and relaxing. Prayer in a traffic jam can do miracles to alleviate irritation and frustration. I believe that prayer incorporated in everyday duties is an excellent resource. I wish it was used more in business, psychological treatment – everywhere where decisions about other people's lives or governmental policies are made!'

One of the things that prevents me from praying more is a belief I picked up from somewhere that God is not really interested in the trivial elements that make up the bulk of my day to day life. If I exclude my present concerns from acceptable conversational topics, I am left with things that are huge and important and seem to require a longer, more official prayer, which I will probably not get round to saying anyway. Deciding that I could talk to God about *anything* meant that I prayed a lot more.

Beholding the Lord

Jeanne Guyon advises using a verse or phrase from Scripture to quiet your mind and help you become aware of the presence of God. The first time I tried this I used Psalm 63 verse 1: 'You, God, are my God, earnestly I seek you.' I had expected to fail miserably at turning away distractions, but it was actually just a question of discipline and concentration, and the reward was that I did honestly sense that I was in God's presence, wordlessly and effortlessly enjoying myself. The beauty of this method is that there is no stress about making sure you have a correct image of who you are in your head. I said earlier that one of the things that has hindered me the most in prayer is anxiety about whether I have the right concept of God in mind. Madame Guyon speaks directly to this, and her words have helped me profoundly these last few days:

'Dear child of God, all your concepts of what God is like really amount to nothing. Do not try to imagine what God is like. Instead, simply believe in his presence.'[4]

You'd think that if I'd discovered this new and delightful way to pray, that I'd take every opportunity to indulge. Actually, I wasted many little windows of time that I could have used to 'behold the Lord' and instead beheld rubbish TV programmes or took sneaky naps or did half-hearted toy-tidying. I can only say that I am frustrated with myself for this, and I share it to make you feel better if you also struggle to choose the right way of spending those precious moments of spare time. My friend Jen says this:

'As a mum with small children, there are always demands that need to be met and it's very easy to just keep going and forget how to stop. If there is a rare occasion to rest and spend some quality time with God there's a niggling suggestion in my mind that I ought to be doing something productive, and before I know it my chance has gone and

*I'm still moving. Sometimes I just don't desire God and so find any
effort to spend time in prayer very hard work.'*

It occurs to me too, that any prayer is better than none. I have a basil
plant on the kitchen window sill. Every few days it looks like it is an ex-
basil plant, headed for the great compost heap in the sky. The amazing
thing is that an hour after I take pity on it and give it some water it
starts looking perky and edible once more. Could it be that prayer can
revive us in the same way?

The Examen

This was a helpful exercise on the nights I remembered to do it. It is a lot
more productive than mulling over the day and dwelling on all the things
you wished you'd done differently or got around to accomplishing. When
I went to bed happy it helped me to pinpoint what had gone well and to
thank God, and it also helped me identify a couple of things that were
causing me generalised disquiet. I think it would be a good habit to get
into, and I am hoping to persevere with it. Shawn, Alexa and I did it over
dinner a couple of times too, and we all heard about each other's days in
a much deeper way than usual as a result.

Week Two

The prayer projects for this week are to focus on praying for others (the
technical and important sounding word for this being **intercession** and
making the fabric of my life into prayer, the **prayer of the ordinary**.

Intercession

While I was at university, I led a Bible study group for the Christian
Union. Every Thursday afternoon, all the group leaders had to attend
an event called Slobs – Study Leaders' Own Bible Study – during which
we were told the correct answers to any questions that our group
members might ask. I am generally suspicious of any theological

statement that can fit onto a bookmark, and I used to challenge some of the tidy orthodoxies that I was instructed to feed my group. I would be told firmly, 'That is a coffee-time question Jo', which was a nice Christian way of saying 'Shut up!' It was during Slobs that I was taught that 'We Cannot Change God's Mind'. If we can't change God's mind, then an answered prayer is when we coincidentally pray for something to happen that God had planned to do anyway. For a long time, this took the wind out of my interceding sails. I realise that this is a complex subject, and that there are many valid positions you could take, but I found this particular position extremely demotivating, and it was with a great sense of relief that I came across the account of God's discussions with Moses about the Israelites.

According to the story, if it weren't for Moses' intercession on behalf of the Israelites, their history would have concluded at some point during Exodus 32 something like this: 'And God wiped the whole wretched bunch off the face of the planet. The End.' As it was, God listened to Moses when he argued that the Egyptians would think badly of God if he destroyed the Israelites (v 12) and reminded him that he had made a promise to Abraham, Isaac and Israel (v 13). By verse 14 'the Lord relented and did not bring on his people the disaster that he had threatened.' Seems to me a pretty clear case of God changing his mind as a result of human intercession.

Now that I subscribe to the belief that prayer makes a difference, the task of intercession equates with work. Perhaps that is why I am so bad at doing it. I find it easy to throw out the phrase 'I'll pray for you', but not so easy to keep the promise. My friend Louise told me that she has stopped saying it, even though it is a cultural expectation among Christians, because she feels that awkward honesty is better than pretence. Personally I think that we mostly have every intention to pray when we offer to, and it can be comforting to people to think that we are doing so even if we don't get round to it.

Take a moment to call to mind your doings of the last few days. Chances are you accumulated several items for your prayer agenda – a job interview, an operation, a marriage in jeopardy, a child's first day at a new school and perhaps a few news items that have tugged at your heart strings unusually strongly. Have you carried the weight of these people and situations as you've gone about your days? Have you brought them to God's attention with the urgency of someone who knows that their words might make a crucial difference? There are so *many* things to pray for. The preacher George Buttrick recommends praying first for our enemies, followed by our leaders, the needy, our friends, and finally our loved ones. This could turn into a full-time job. It is going to be a busy week.[5]

I am not aware of any particular enemies in my life at the moment, and England's leaders are about to change (there is an election approaching at the time of writing this) so I started by praying for those I have a particular duty to pray for – my godchildren, my family, the people I have told I would pray for lately. Then, thick and fast, other concerns began to need airtime. A close friend found out her mother has cancer. My neighbours are Tamil, and are suffering greatly knowing their family members are in extreme danger in Sri Lanka – the news this week has been a constant reminder of their need for God's comfort. I spoke with a friend who works for a wonderful charity in the North East of England and she told me she faces the possibility of redundancy and the end of the incredibly fruitful work done by the organisation, due to hugely strained finances. Another friend gave birth last Monday to a beautiful little girl with a distressing health issue. I began to feel a bit overwhelmed, and ashamed that it has taken the motivation of this 'experiment' to get me on my knees on behalf of the need all around me.

While intercession can feel like work, it is also one of the great blessings of being a Christian. There is something we can do in the face of suffering other than stand there fretfully wringing our hands. We can take our hopes and anxieties about that situation to the Almighty God, knowing our prayers are heard, and that if anyone can do anything about it, he can. I used to have a wooden cross in my room, two bits of driftwood tied together with a silk scarf, and I'd write the names of people I knew who needed prayer on bits of paper and pin them to the wood. It was a visual reminder that I had carried them to Jesus and he had them in his care.

There is a lady in her seventies living in the North of England who prays for my family. I have never even met her, but she took us on about twenty years ago and has prayed in great detail and with total commitment ever since. My mother writes to her with updates and she gets on her knees on our behalf. Perhaps one day I'll sit with Jesus in heaven and he'll fill me in on the influence her prayers had on my life. Who knows – maybe she is part of the reason I am there having that conversation at all…

Ordinary prayer

The big quandary of the week was how to make the Wednesday morning ordeal of my mums and toddlers group into a prayerful and God-glorifying occasion. I find it an ordeal because there are over a hundred bodies large and small swarming around the room, putting the bones in the small ear under significant strain, and, more than that, some of the mothers remind me of the people I was at school with who made me feel inferior and inappropriately dressed! Alexa doesn't like it either, and clings to my leg, whimpering, which tries my patience. The situation only really allows for small talk, which I don't enjoy and certainly don't excel at, particularly when it calls for discussing shopping, shoes or skiing. It is altogether very trying, and I totally failed in my mission to make it more meaningful this week.

Debriefing with my friend Ally afterwards, she asked me what it would look like for me to glorify God in that situation. I think what I'd like is to look out for lonely people and make their experience of the morning less lonely, rather than feeling sorry for myself for being left out. I'd like to demonstrate the fruits of the spirit, most especially patience towards my daughter. I'd like to be more servant-minded and be the person to do the bulk of the clearing up, with a cheerful attitude. I'd like to have confidence in the knowledge that I belong to Jesus, and not mind that I do not have flawless make-up and a huge house. I think these situations are where the depth of our spirituality is truly put to the test. I am sure you have your Tiny Tots equivalent, be it your book club, your office environment, your neighbours or your extended family. These places where we are tested are potentially schools of Ordinary Prayer. I deserve a C minus this week, but I intend to keep trying to improve my grade, believe me.

Week Three

I am going to pray using an Anglican prayer book this week, following the prayers for morning and evening. I know that many people find this a wonderful aid to conversation with God, and I am keen to give it a go. In the past I've found it difficult to engage with formal liturgy. I've tended to read it rather than pray it, and be rather relieved when I've got to the concluding bits. But if I can push through my bad attitude and approach this with an open mind, I can see there could be a lot to be gained. How amazing to pray the same words along with centuries of believers, as well as others from my own time. It will be good for me to have some discipline and structure, and I will definitely benefit from being reminded twice daily of truths about God's character and actions in the world. Perhaps it will save Jesus some work making my prayers acceptable before God if someone else has written them! So much care and thought has gone into crafting the language and the theology behind it.

Using a prayer book

I was slightly concerned about how I'd manage to find time for the Morning Prayer. I have a friend who gets up *before* her three little children in order to spend time with God. I am in awe of people whose spiritual lives impact on their sleep allowance. I have a long way to go in my journey to holiness before you'll find me on my knees any earlier than I absolutely have to be out of bed. Currently my daughter functions as my alarm clock. She is not a very good one – she goes off too early, and seems to have been made without a snooze bar. Come October I'll have two alarms, just in case there was any danger that I might find a way to sleep through Alexa's efforts. So with that time slot unavailable I have had to be a little creative. Morning Prayer has happened while eating cereal, over the noise of children's TV, during lunch time naps, and sitting on the floor in the middle of a pile of colourful building blocks. Today, the last official day, has been the most civilised, since my distracting charge is with her childminder.

Evening Prayer has been easier to manage, and my routine has been to come downstairs from putting Alexa to bed and head straight for the red book with the multicoloured ribbon book marks.

For those of you unfamiliar with this particular prayer book, let me introduce you to the format. There are different prayers for each day of the week, but the layout is pretty much the same, at least in 'ordinary time'. Ordinary time, let me enlighten you, is 'the Monday after the Sunday on which Candlemas has been observed until Shrove Tuesday, and again from the Monday after Pentecost until Morning Prayer on the day before All Saints' Day.'[6] So now you know.

It begins with Preparation. In the morning you say, 'Oh Lord, open our lips and our mouth shall proclaim your praise.' In the evening, you say, 'O God, make speed to save us. O Lord, make haste to help us.' It struck me halfway through the week that the morning preparation is a comforting recognition that we need God's help to praise him, and that we can't do it at all if he doesn't step in and make it possible by opening our mouths. Looking back now another thought occurs: the times I did these prayers vocally (as opposed to reading them silently) were far more meaningful. Is there perhaps something significant in proclaiming praise out loud, even in a private time of devotion? This is just one example of how words that passed me by in a superficial kind of way came to strike me more profoundly through repetition, and I can imagine one of the real benefits of making the use of a prayer book a regular practice.

The main body of the prayers is Bible readings interspersed with silence, set prayers and refrains, and always the Lord's Prayer. Content-wise, it was very nourishing – the spiritual equivalent of a chunky muesli full of nuts, fruits and grains and doing you a world of good even if a little hard work to chew on lazy mornings. It gives you the scope of the entire story of salvation twice a day, and is packed full of sound doctrine and truth. But not only that. You have the opportunity to begin the day requesting, 'May the light of your presence, O God, set our hearts on fire with love for you.' Surely this is a prayer God would want to answer, and if we really are able to pray it and not just say the words on the page, what a difference that could make to a day.

I wasn't entirely won over though. It seems very much geared for corporate use, with certain lines designated to be said by 'All', and the personal pronouns all plural. I had my father to stay on Thursday night, and when he and I did it together it seemed more apt. That was the time I found I appropriated the words most deeply and they became our prayers, said with real reverence. This morning I press-ganged Shawn into doing it with me, and again, it was a lovely time of meeting with God in the company of another believer. But when I talked to my friend Kate about this, she challenged me to use my historical and geographical imagination – while I may be alone in the room with the prayer book, around the world and through the ages I am in the company of others praying the same words. She has a point.

The times when I went through the service alone were mixed. To be fair, I have to blame this entirely on my own attitude. There is little point in dragging your eyes over a printed page just to fulfil a duty and to be able to say you did it, and sometimes that is exactly what I did. But even on those occasions, pinpricks of light would pierce the holes in the blackout-blinds of my mind. Can you be entirely unmoved by words such as, 'The glorious grace of God is freely bestowed on us in the Beloved' (Evening Prayer on Monday) or 'Shine on us, O God, who dwell in darkness, and guide us into the way of peace.' (Evening Prayer on Saturday)?

There were two themes running through this week which definitely impacted my prayer life, and I think they are relevant enough to mention. The first was that through sheer disorganisation I missed six days of my anti-depressant medication, and consequently found I had some interesting physical and emotional symptoms to deal with. In fact, it wasn't just me who had to deal with them: apologies all round! It took me a while to twig that my outlook on life was driven by brain chemistry and before it did, I found myself thinking blackly that my ability to pray is similar to that of a frog's (no offence to frogs), that God doesn't like me anyway, and that knowing God hasn't made any difference to my character flaws, so probably I don't know God at all. Maybe when I thought I did, I *actually* knew someone else, like a Star Trek character I'd once seen on TV.

My point is that there are factors that influence how we feel about prayer that might be skewing our perspective somewhat. For me this was going cold turkey from long-term medication. For you it might be that you have a newborn and haven't slept more than an hour-and-a-half in a row for the last seven weeks. Or it might be that you have that bug that's been going round. Or that your house is on the market. You get my drift? Nothing works in isolation, so take note of the reasons you might not feel so great about praying and persevere through your feelings about it. Alternatively, like my friend Ben, you might pray the most when you are stressed or low.

The other theme was that I spent a lot of time with my Tamil neighbours this week. There is a war going on in Sri Lanka and they have several family members trapped in the conflict zone. They feel passionately that their people should have their own state and the right to rule themselves, and they are strong supporters of the Tamil Tigers. It has been complicated trying to be their friends through this time – reports on the news are primarily coming from Sinhalese government sources, and are radically different from the version I am getting from next door. I wanted to show them I cared; I went with them to a demonstration in London, and read all the literature they gave me, and listened to the outpourings of anger – and I have prayed. It has been hard to know what to pray. What would it look like if God's will was done on that bit of earth as in heaven? I suppose that is not my question to answer. Mostly I have prayed that Raj's brother and his family will be safe and that I will somehow manage to convey that Jesus loves them and is with them in their pain. They are Hindus, so this is tricky. I have been immensely grateful that I can take my thoughts and my feelings of inadequacy to God, and know that he loves my neighbours far more than I ever could.

Week Four

The challenge this week is unceasing prayer. This is the Everest of spiritual tasks and it seems a little ludicrous to attempt it for just seven days. I suppose that really it is the ultimate goal of a godly life, to be in constant communion with the Trinity, and I don't plan to give up when the week is done. I anticipate that it is going to be hard and that I am initially going to do extremely badly. Because of this, I am also going to have a 'sub-challenge' that I am likely to find easier which is to journal my prayers for a week. This is something that I have done on and off since I was eleven, although it has been sporadic at best since I became a mother. I'm looking forward to getting back into it.

Unceasing prayer

There is no way I came close to a week of non-stop prayer, but I have to say that if you aim for that, you certainly pray more often than you would otherwise. My approach was simply to turn my thoughts God-ward as often as it occurred to me to do so. I wanted to see if I could spend as much time as I could consciously in his presence, and it was a really great exercise. Brother Lawrence, a French monk who lived in the seventeenth century, was the best known practitioner of this form of prayer, and his letters on practising the presence of God are incredibly inspiring. Here is an excerpt from one of them:

'I have abandoned all my forms of worship, and those prayers which are not obligatory, and I do nothing else but abide in his holy presence, and I do this by a simple attentiveness and an habitual, loving, turning of my eyes on him. This I should call the actual presence of God, or to put it better, a wordless and secret conversation between the soul and God which no longer ends.'[7]

The question is, why if we can live our lives in God's presence, do we not do it? I suppose it feels like work to get our minds into a new habit. And we are fallen people, who, in seeking holiness, have to fight strong natural inclinations to be naughty and horrible. Amanda, a housewife and mother says this:

'When I pray, I love it! I find it hard to imagine why I don't do it all the time. Life seems to get in the way, and I find it frustrating that I'm not developing my relationship with God more steadily. Laziness, busyness and having the wrong priorities all seem to stop me praying more.'

I can relate to that very closely, I don't know about you. But life lived with God is incomparable to life lived any other way, and I am determined to make this practice a long-term habit of mind.

Journaling

I appreciated the times I spent getting my thoughts and prayers on paper this week. It slowed me down and kept my mind from wandering, and looking back over what I had written later was interesting. Actually it made me cringe, and I only read a couple of entries! I tried to journal with Alexa around at first, but we ended up fighting over the pen, and then I had to find other windows of time which wasn't altogether easy. I don't know whether you find the idea of journaling appealing, but here are some ideas of things you could jot down:

- the people and situations you have on your mind
- long-hand prayers as you pray them
- Bible verses that have spoken to you and quotes from books you are reading that you want to remember
- anything you think God might have said to you lately
- worries or concerns
- lists of things you want to give thanks for.

One last thing on journaling: in my experience, the nicer the journal, the less likely I am to use it. The only journals I ever filled up from front to back page were tatty old school exercise books. I have multitudes of hardbacked, beautiful, sacred-looking volumes that are only a quarter full. I am not sure why that is, but my advice is don't splash out on a really great book, just start with any old notebook you have lying around.

A Conversation with Pete Greig

A few days ago I headed into central London to have a chat with the founder of 24-7 Prayer, a movement that has people praying around the clock in 100 countries. Pete Greig is apparently on a list somewhere of the top 50 revolutionary leaders of his generation, has written several totally brilliant books, is the director of prayer at Holy Trinity Brompton, and has been an extremely hands-on father to his two boys. It would be fair to say that I approached our meeting not a little star-struck. It didn't help that I had spent the last few days reading things he has written, and forgot that although I now know *him* really well, he has never met *me*, so as well as being sycophantic in a way that humble people find very uncomfortable, I was also creepily over-familiar. Add to this the fact that my jazzy recording device is apparently no use without a 'card' in it, whatever that is, and there was a little awkwardness to overcome. It turned out that Pete had a friend sitting in the same hotel lobby with a Dictaphone in his pocket, so you can, against the odds, hear our whole discussion on the podcast at www.scriptureunion.org.uk/godhunting, and laugh at me embarrassing myself!

I began by asking him what happens to his prayer life on the days he has full charge of his small sons. Pete's wife Samie has epilepsy and although he says things have improved for her lately, she has suffered years of seizures that medication has been unable to control, and he has had to play a very active parenting role as a result.

'I still find prayer very difficult and yet something that I'm always wanting to grow in. I think that one of the keys for me is to try and see prayer as something embedded in normality not removed from it. There's a lovely old Celtic prayer that says 'I make this bed in the name of the Father, the Son and the Holy Spirit.' Too much of our understanding of spirituality has been shaped by people living cloistered lives without kids and school runs and whatever else.'

But before, like me, you breathe a sigh of relief and think you have a prayer-pro's sanction to abandon attempts to find dedicated and focused prayer slots, keep listening:

'It is important to carve intentional time out so that you can re-centre on Jesus and then live the rest of your life more aware of his presence.'

Pete thinks he has got things wrong on a regular basis, but has had moments that stand out to him when the concept of prayer in and through the ordinary has really hit home, one of which he spoke about in slightly gruesome detail!

'One of the times when I think I got it right was when my wife was very sick and I was her primary carer. We were doing a season of 24/7 prayer and I was down for a 3am prayer slot, which I needed like a hole in the head. I remember taking Danny who was just a baby in nappies into the prayer room with me and he started to scream and yell, and this was meant to be my time with God and he was spoiling it. I had a choice then, either to decide that my child was this demon child trying to take me away from God or that somehow God wanted to meet with me in the screaming, which didn't seem very spiritual. He was screaming because he needed his nappy changing. I very deliberately started changing his nappy as an act of prayer. I know it sounds really peculiar, but pulling it off, and the horrible smell hitting me and seeing that nasty looking gunk babies churn out, I very deliberately started thinking about sin and the rubbish I produce and how it defiles me, and cleaning him I was confessing and thinking about how God makes us clean. Sorry for a bit of a base analogy, but I think if we can't find God in the real stuff of life like that then we will only find him in the cloisters where there are squirrels and rainbows.'

One of Pete's books, *God on Mute*,[8] deals with the tricky subject of unanswered prayer. I was told once that God always answers prayer; he says 'yes', 'no' or 'not yet'. How very tidy and simple that makes everything seem. As I thought about what I wanted to ask Pete, I realised that my issue at the moment is less to do with unanswered prayer, and more to do with the fact that sometimes prayer is answered. This means we can get our hopes up in the face of desperate circumstances, and for me it seems easier to face the worst. He agreed with me that miracles are pretty arbitrary, but insisted that we must keep asking for them. If we don't turn to God in desperate situations, where do we go? He doesn't believe that unanswered prayer should make us question God's character or goodness.

'It is not so much about the mystery of God – he has revealed himself fully in Jesus – but more about the mystery of creation, which is infinitely complex, profoundly fallen and yet being reconciled as we speak, according to Romans 8 and 2 Corinthians 5. So we live in a very confusing created order, and we are in a spiritual battle. God doesn't get his will done all the time I don't believe, although he will ultimately... We're engaged in a battle against evil that needs to be fought through the courts, through law enforcement, through good parenting and spiritually through prayer.'

I found this a very convincing argument, and in line with what I want to believe about the authenticity of the relationship it is possible to have with the living God. I was relieved to hear him say that:

'I am absolutely certain that our prayers are not just a dress rehearsal or a mirror of what God was going to do anyway in advance. If that is our theology we won't really ever pray. We'll only pray out of legalistic obedience. We have to maintain if we read the gospels that miracles happen and if we don't pray about some things they will not happen, and it's as serious as that. Prayer at its essence is partnering with God in ruling and reigning over the earth. It's coming into alignment with his will and agreement with his people and therefore we are making decisions with God in prayer.'

The implications of that are scary. If certain things only happen as a result of prayer, we have a huge responsibility to pray, and an infinite range of people and circumstances to pray about. Was I about to fall headlong into a guilt-trip trap? Before I could spin into a full-blown panic, Pete gave me a perspective that restored me to calm.

'There are six billion of us and an infinite number of needs, so we cannot be driven by the needs; we have to be driven by the Holy Spirit speaking to us and putting particular people and situations on our hearts. With the Haiti earthquake recently, I had a girl come to me and say, "I don't understand what's happening to me, but whenever I see coverage on the TV, I weep. What is that? I've watched other disasters unfold without that happening." And I said to her, "I think that's God giving you his broken heart and it's a call to intercede."'

The other morning there was a report from Northern Sudan on Radio 4, in which a woman recounted how she had fled a raid just hours after giving birth, with her newborn and her toddler. Her toddler was killed as they ran. Because I am at a similar stage of motherhood, her story has stuck with me, and I have felt compelled to pray for her. I asked Pete if there was any validity to my prayers if I was not at the same time trying to track her down and doing something concrete to make a difference to her situation. I slightly expected him to answer that my prayers were perfectly concrete enough, but I was not to be let off the hook that easily. He eyeballed me across the now-empty tea pot and said:

'You will have to ask God if you are to be a part of the answer to your prayers for that woman.'

Pete has confirmed my suspicions that prayer is an exciting and risky endeavour, with real life implications and unpredictable consequences. I have a lot to think about on my way home.

Reflections

I have loved this month of prayer, and it has made me realise that time is really not the main issue when it comes to the reasons for not praying. I don't pray because prayer is hard work. I don't pray because I am in a spiritual battle and there are forces of evil out there that do not want me to be praying. I don't pray because I find the whole thing bewildering and mysterious, and I don't pray because I'm afraid nothing will happen as a result. And sometimes I don't pray because in moments when my belief in God is robust, I know that what might happen could be dramatic, and I am not sure I'm up for drama, even holy, wonderful drama. But giving up on prayer is not an option for me, so I must keep working at this business of communicating with God.

CHAPTER TWO:

FASTING

Jesus, full of the Holy Spirit, left the Jordan and was led by the Spirit into the wilderness, where for forty days he was tempted by the devil. He ate nothing during those days, and at the end of them he was hungry. The devil said to him, 'If you are the Son of God, tell this stone to become bread.' Jesus answered, 'It is written: "People do not live on bread alone."'

LUKE 4:1–4

I have not been particularly excited about experimenting with fasting. I wonder if I will be more enthusiastic by the end of the month. I need a better understanding of what it should ideally achieve, because thus far I have been secretly pleased that a bi-product of fasting from food is weight loss. Being female, I have a somewhat complicated relationship with all things edible, which I realise is a shockingly sexist thing to say, and if you are a female without food issues, do get in touch and rant at me. I am not holding my breath, because I do not believe you exist. It is hard for me to approach calorie reduction on a spiritual level, because as well as the weight loss factor, there is the high that results from exerting self-control, the low that comes from removing a major source of pleasure and comfort from my day, and the desire for lots of people to know and be impressed by my self-denial. On top of all this, I get extremely agitated and irritable if a meal is late, let alone missing, and I certainly don't feel inclined to pray.

I know that typically fasting is gastronomic. If a Christian you know lets slip that they are fasting[1], it would be fair to assume that they are not eating for a period of time, for the purpose of creating more time for prayer, and seeking God in a particularly intentional way. Food is something of which we very immediately and intensely feel the lack. The physical response strips us of our defences. A food fast might reveal some unpleasant character traits that our well-fed selves are able to hide. We then have the opportunity to come to God with our newly acquired self-knowledge and ask him to forgive and transform us. Fasting from food reminds us that the deepest sustenance is that which we receive from God. When Jesus was tempted by Satan in the desert at the end of a forty day fast, though famished, he was able to resist turning stones into bread because he knew that 'people do not live on bread alone, but on every word that comes from the mouth of God' (Matthew 4:4). When Jesus talked about fasting, he was talking about abstaining from food, and this is the primary reason that a normal fast involves missing meals. His teaching assumes that his followers will fast, and that it is a normal part of devotion to God, along with prayer and giving. In Matthew 6:16–18 Jesus says, 'When you fast....', presupposing that his disciples will be carrying out this discipline and in Matthew 9:15, he says the guests of the bridegroom will fast when he is taken away from them, meaning he assumes that his followers will fast again after he has left.

However clear the biblical call to fast may be, we seem to have far more trouble accepting it as an aspect of Christian devotion than giving away money, which the majority of Christians do unquestioningly. It may be that in affluent societies, financial generosity does not involve much sacrifice, whereas hunger hurts. I confess this has been one of the major deterrents for me – it just seems too costly.

How has fasting featured in my life until this point? Not very significantly. When I was going through an ultra-religious phase in my early teens, I fasted from lunch one day a week. I don't really remember if this was for any particular purpose, or if it impacted how I related to God. I expect I was pretty grumpy by supper time, and I recall feeling very pleased with myself for doing it. I have done two or three '24-hour famines' with World Vision, where the idea is to raise sponsorship for the hungry in the world, and forgo food for a day in solidarity. Last year I fasted for a day with two friends because we wanted to pray with particular urgency for another friend. Over a few Lent seasons I have joined the masses in giving up chocolate, but more as a general exercise in discipline than as a spiritual practice. I'd really like to do better in the future.

Having made the case for fasting from food, I now need to tell you that the fasts I will be doing this month actually have nothing to do with food. As I write, I am nineteen weeks pregnant and a food fast would be unfair on my tiny dependant. I still believe however, that I will have a valid experience of fasting. There are some situations when food cannot be foregone, pregnancy being one, ill health another, eating disorders another and so on, but everyone can gain the spiritual benefits of fasting with a little creativity.

I have chosen different things to go without each week – fiction, hot drinks, media and sugar. These are all things that are important to me, and feature significantly in my life on a daily basis. The Old Testament laws on sacrifice all put heavy emphasis on giving to the Lord the very best – the healthiest lambs, the first fruits of the crop, the most flawless goat in the herd. It is in that spirit that I have tried to decide what to go without. If for some reason you are not willing or able to do a traditional food fast, here are some other ideas for fasts:

A clothes fast
I am not suggesting you go naked, but rather forgo the acquisition of new items for your wardrobe for a while. A friend of mine does this every

other year, for the entire year, and finds it a meaningful and important spiritual exercise. I'm not sure it would be a hardship for me – I hate shopping.

A carbon fast
Good stewardship of the planet is a part of our worship to the God who made it, loves it and grieves over the damage we do to it. Our energy use directly impacts the poor of the world, who feel most acutely the effects of climate change. During Lent 2009, many people in England took part in a carbon fast instigated by the charity Tear Fund, who produced a list of daily actions, available at *www.tearfund.org/carbonfast09*.

A telephone fast
I didn't consider this myself, because it would be a joy to me to give up the telephone for any length of time. My mobile is never charged and I can rarely find it when I need it, which is not often. I am perfectly comfortable leaving our home phone to ring if we have company, and when I have a call to make I put it on my 'to do' list where it sits until the last possible moment. This is not the way everyone sees the telephone, and so I include it here for your consideration.

I may not be fasting from food, but I expect that tackling other things in life that I am dependent on, or perhaps even addicted to, will be an equally profound spiritual experience. There are things that we all do to comfort ourselves, address our anxiety, fill our silences, when it is God we should turn to in need. I am planning to make myself vulnerable by removing the props I usually rely on, and I hope I am able to lean more heavily on God and not just reach for new props.

Week One

The fiction fast
Some of you might wonder whether giving up fiction is a bit of a cop-out, and perhaps not sacrificial enough to warrant inclusion. Let me try

and explain the place of fiction in my life. I have just brought downstairs the pile of novels I have by my bed. These are books I have consumed in the past few weeks, or am currently part-way through:

Empress Orchid by Anchee Min
Three by Flannery O'Connor
The Running Mate by Joe Klein
London by Edward Rutherfurd
Suite Française by Irène Némirovsky
The Road Home by Rose Tremain
Happenstance by Carol Shields
Slam by Nick Hornby
The Island by Victoria Hislop
The Righteous Men by Sam Bourne

I am not at a stage in my life when opportunities to get lost in a book present themselves readily, so the fact that I still get through so many shows my dedication. I read before I go to sleep, I read on the toilet, I read if Alexa gets distracted by her plastic kitchen and forgets to involve me in her playing for a few minutes, I read on trains, in doctors' waiting rooms and at airports. If I don't have a good book on the go, I feel a bit fidgety and dissatisfied. Fiction provides me with an alternative universe or two to inhabit, and in that sense is unhealthy escapism. If I am really engrossed in a particular book then I think and dream about the characters as though they are real. I could argue that it expands my horizons, gives me insights into different perspectives, improves my vocabulary, and is a very enjoyable and wholesome way to relax, and those arguments are persuasive because they are all true. But I know that my calling is primarily to embrace my own life as it is, in the here and now, and a week of confining myself within my own reality will be beneficial.

I may be a voracious reader, but I have allowed myself to become a little lazy in my reading habits. Back when I was a theology student, a good eighty per cent of my reading was edifying, nourishing and demanding. I have felt a growing sense of unease at my neglect of books that might do me some good, and by denying myself fiction, I will by necessity be thrown their way again. Their pitiful cries as I pass them by on the shelf will at last be heeded! On reflection though, I think that mothers of young children have a good excuse not to be reading Kierkegaard before dropping off to sleep – we should really be commended for focusing our bleary eyes on any printed page at all, especially if it is one with no pictures.

There are several reasons why giving up fiction this week is going to be particularly hard. I am going up to Liverpool for a speaking engagement, and will be on the train for three hours each way – a rare opportunity for uninterrupted indulgence in a novel. What's more, I am in the middle of reading *London* by Edward Rutherfurd, which, while not exactly great literature, is nonetheless gripping, and I have a new book by Anne Tyler, an author I usually enjoy greatly, waiting in the wings. Lastly, I have been struggling to get to sleep lately, and reading fiction has always helped me wind down.

Somehow it seems important that this is going to cost me. Lauren Winner, in her book *Girl Meets God*, recounts a sermon she had heard on Ash Wednesday, the start of Lent, which gave her a new insight into the meaning of fasting. The preacher had said it was important to give up something truly of yourself, something that matters, and that the spirit in which it is given is what makes the gesture meaningful. He encouraged his congregation to think about receiving a gift from a friend:

'Say your friend has a beautiful green sundress. You have liked and admired that sundress for months. She gives it to you. If it's just a cast-off – she has eighteen others just like it, so giving it to you is no real sacrifice – the whole exchange feels a little anti-climactic. But if your friend loves that dress too, loves it dearly but wants you to have

it because she knows it will make you happy, then you are thrilled. The dress takes on a whole new meaning.'[2]

I am hoping that timing my fiction fast to coincide with some prime reading time will make God happy…

A week later…
I am just at the beginning of the whole fasting experiment, and I have to confess I don't think my understanding of its purpose runs very deep yet. I managed to stay off the fiction this week, withstanding some SERIOUS temptation, but I'm not sure of the spiritual significance of the exercise. The worst times were before I went to sleep. I ended up reading a hefty book on marriage and dipped in and out of *The Purpose Driven Life* by Rick Warren, but they weren't at all what I felt like reading, and I got a bit grumpy. I did find that I was more likely to pray as I fell asleep because I wasn't mulling over the people and events of my book, and I know that is definitely a good thing to have come from the week. My mind was freed up to focus on God, and that is what I mostly tried to do when I would have otherwise been reading. Even the discomfort was somewhat useful; it served as a reminder to turn my mind to prayer. Those of my friends who fast regularly from food say that hunger pangs function in the same way. I could have done more to use the time I would have otherwise been reading fiction for prayer. One of the key ideas behind doing a fast is to free up space for being with God in a more leisurely way than usual, over mealtimes if you are giving up food. I think if I try this again, the way to go would be to fast from reading of all kinds and not just fiction, and to be more intentional about using reading time as prayer time.

There was an unexpected advantage to my lack of easy-reading matter on one of my train journeys. I had brought *The Divine Conspiracy* by Dallas Willard with me but it was sitting unopened next to me. Ten minutes after we pulled out of London Euston the man opposite me had a call with the news that the 18-year-old son of a family friend had committed suicide that morning. If I had been buried in a gripping novel I might have been too preoccupied to eavesdrop, and then unavailable to offer comfort. We talked for two hours, and I think he found our conversation helpful. The hole fiction leaves in my life has the potential to be a useful space if I allow God to help me fill it.

What has become apparent over these few days is that I use fiction to avoid boredom. I want to find out what lies beneath the boredom, because living in fear of space and quiet and my own company is not healthy. I am sure this is going to be a major issue when I have my month looking at the discipline of solitude.

Week Two

The hot drink fast

Recently, my friend Julia stopped drinking coffee. Many people give up coffee for health reasons, but Julia has given it up because she thinks that God asked her to. She told me that when she had become a Christian aged nineteen, she left many things behind and, thinking she was doing really well, asked God whether there was anything else that had to go. Coffee apparently. Now in her early forties, not only had she continued to drink coffee, but she had become known as a person who loved coffee. Now that she has been obedient, she feels a block has been removed in her relationship with God. Although coffee drinking hardly counts as a debauched habit, for her it symbolised her independent and rebellious spirit. As Sampson lost his spiritual strength and effectiveness when his hair was cut, so she feels that she is somehow weakened when she drinks coffee. To me, this says a lot about how insidiously innocent things can undermine our closeness to God.

Hot drinks are the punctuation marks in my days. Tea is usually the second, if not the first thought I have when I wake up each morning. I get Alexa from her cot, shuffle downstairs and put the kettle on. That first cup of the day is the best. I enjoy every steaming, fragrant moment. Then around eleven my inner coffee alert goes off. I will have been anticipating the mid-morning pause with pleasure, and if I'm at home I will make coffee in my Italian stove-top coffee pot with hot, frothy milk and drink it in my tall pottery Portuguese mug. Mmmm. Last time I was pregnant I couldn't stand coffee, but this time I'm still enjoying my daily fix. Then at four o' clock, along with the rest of the English population, I put the kettle on again for my afternoon tea. This is best shared with friends, and is usually accompanied by phrases such as 'Aaah – this hits the spot!' and 'I could have murdered for this cup of tea!'. That is usually me done for the day. You might think this is quite moderate caffeine consumption, but you must understand that a minimum of three hot drinks a day is non-negotiable. I have never even thought of attempting to mess with this routine. The thought of it kind of terrifies me actually which is why it is an obvious candidate for a fast.

The week-long headache

This week was about as hard as I expected it to be, with the addition of a protracted headache that I perhaps should have anticipated. The headache has been a blight on the week, and only let up when I gave in and had a coke for the caffeine, which I did on three days out of the seven. It has been a little sobering to realise how dependent my body has become on this substance. I knew I was psychologically addicted, but I have been dealing with some very strong physical cravings too. At times during this week I have been a bit preoccupied with how my body felt. I have wondered how to make sure that this fasting I am attempting is a spiritual exercise, and not just a way of proving to myself that I can be disciplined if I try. Having done two weeks now, I can see that tackling my dependency on certain things is revealing plenty of uncomfortable truths. The question is whether I take the opportunity to bring these revelations to God and allow him to deal with them, or whether I just hold out until the fast is over and go back to how I was before.

There were several moments when I was severely tempted to give up. I spoke at a women's breakfast on Saturday, which involved sitting in a room full of tea and coffee drinking women – oh how I envied them! And I knew that just a small cup would deal with my sore head. I even began to say to God that I would be able to serve him better through my speaking if I felt better, so did he think I actually should have the tea? But I knew I would have to confess it to you, dear reader, and my pride wouldn't let me touch the beautiful liquid. Another moment came when I arrived at my friend Ally's house at 4 o clock to find our two cups waiting for us on the kitchen table, the steam rising heavenwards in the afternoon sun. How easy it would have been to take a little sip.

The cravings have played a role though, in my quest to make this a spiritual exercise. They have been a constant reminder that I am 'fasting', and in the discomfort and frustration of it I have been talking to God about how much I rely on him. I would love to crave the presence of the Lord in a similarly urgent way to the way I've craved my tea and coffee, and I rarely do. Psalm 42 verses 1 and 2 say:

As the deer pants for streams of water,
  so my soul pants for you, my God.
My soul thirsts for God, for the living God.
  When can I go and meet with God?

Trivial as it sounds, going without hot drinks has given me some insight into what a true craving for God might look like, and for that alone it has been worthwhile.

Week Three

The media fast

During the coming week, I am planning on going cold turkey on the following key props of my daily life: Internet, radio, television, newspapers and magazines. I am very excited about the fact I am now allowed tea again – that was hard – but this week is going to really stretch me. You may not have understood why I chose fiction for my first fast, and maybe you think that hot drinks are not so essential to health and well being, but I imagine that attempting a media fast is going to finally get me some respect. How would you feel about doing the same thing?

My family did not have a television as I was growing up, which perhaps explains my attachment to reading. In our first few years of marriage Shawn and I worked our way through DVD sets of television series, but never watched live TV. Just recently we bought a licence as you have to do in England, and now have access to whatever junk is being broadcast at any particular time. For me, this has led to a significant amount of time wasted and I don't feel good about it. I am not the only one who feels a bit guilty about the amount of time I spend mesmerised by the screen on the wall. Forty nine per cent of Americans apparently feel they also watch too much TV. And I think perhaps they do; at an average of four hours a day, a typical 65-year-old will have spent nine whole years of his life occupied in this way.[3]

The Internet is another crafty time-thief. Teenagers in the UK spend an average of 31 hours a week online[4]. Adults do a bit better, or perhaps just don't answer surveys with the same honesty – they spend 34.4 hours a month on the Internet.[5] I have no idea how much time I spend pottering around cyberspace, but I do know that I am a bit compulsive about my Internet use, and that very little of it is spent doing anything productive or useful. Mostly I spy on people on Facebook, update my website, check my book rankings on Amazon (sad I know!), and look up the baby's progress on a site that has pictures, statistics and information about her weekly developments.

The radio became a part of my life when Alexa was a tiny baby, specifically Radio 4 which is all talk. As my body trudged through the day's grunt work of cleaning, feeding, clothing, comforting and generally maintaining my child, my mind badly needed something to chew on and I was soon hooked on political debates, interviews with playwrights, current affairs and history lessons. The habit remains, and has become company in the car as well as the house now.

Newspapers and magazines are not such a major problem for me, although they are another way I try to avoid boredom and silence so they must be foregone. As a family we have yearly subscriptions to *The Christian Writer*, *The Week*, *Wired*, *Psychologies*, *Red*, and *Youthwork* magazines.

Hard lessons
This week I have felt like a dog that keeps forgetting it is tied up, charges off at full speed and reaching the end of the rope gets its neck yanked. There have been countless times each day that I have instinctively gone to the remote control, my laptop, or the power button on the radio, only to remember with an unpleasant jolt that these things are temporarily out of bounds.

Shawn was away over the weekend, and the very worst moments were once Alexa had gone to bed. I don't think that it would be putting it too strongly to say that I *desperately* wanted to cheat. I got as far as opening the cover of *The Week* and reading a sentence, but I felt sick with myself and stopped. I badly wanted to watch something on TV. I just didn't want to sit in my own company, and I resisted turning to God.

I have not enjoyed the realisation that my behaviour has over time become so out of my own control. I have had to admit to myself that I am more dependent on the noise than I want to be. The apostle Paul talks about the same sensation in relation to the human state of bondage to sin in his letter to the Romans:

I do not understand what I do. For what I want to do, I do not do, but what I hate I do…I know that good itself does not dwell in me, that is, in my sinful nature. For I have the desire to do what is good, but I cannot carry it out…

So I find this law at work: Although I want to do good, evil is right there with me. For in my inner being I delight in God's law; but I see another law at work in me, waging war against the law of my mind and making me a prisoner of the law of sin at work within me. (Romans 7:15–17, 21–23)

In his book *Addiction and Grace*, Gerald May argues that in everyone, religious or not, there is an inborn desire for God. This desire is easily transferred from its true object onto other things, whether people, behaviours or objects which we then become addicted to. Most people think of addiction in terms of dependence on drugs or alcohol, but May contends that: 'The same processes that are responsible for addiction to alcohol and narcotics are also responsible for addiction to ideas, work, relationships, power, moods, fantasies and an endless variety of other things.'[6] He believes that all of us, without exception, suffer from addiction. And he believes that our addictions can lead us, in our helplessness, to a deeper understanding of and appreciation for, grace.

I have come to see this week that I use media to self-medicate in some way – it soothes my discomfort and distracts me. My challenge is to explore the source of the discomfort rather than holding on until the week is up (tomorrow thankfully!) and continuing to avoid it. If the truth is that I have misinterpreted a yearning for God as a yearning for entertainment, then I have been given a chance to take a different direction. That scares me. The paradox is that while I want to grow closer to God, I am also fighting a strong instinct to run away from him. This is the very fight with the sinful self that Paul talks about.

I had a friend from Canada to stay a few days during the week, and she had done a media fast during the previous season of Lent. We had interesting discussions about the impact this had had on her. It was long enough to break some habits and she had changed her behaviour as a result. She inspired me to press on to the end of my pitifully short seven-day stint, and I plan on addressing my media use in the long-term too. For starters I am going to institute Internet-free Sundays.

Week Four

The sugar fast
I eat most of my sugar in the form of cake. I love cake and lately I have been eating too much of it, and eating it for the wrong reasons (boredom, frustration, greed etc). If you know the right reasons for eating cake, please let me know! If there are any guilt-free cake-eaters out there I'd love to join them. Since sugar is banned this week, there will also be no marmalade on my toast, no sweetness in my coffee and no chocolate, ice cream, biscuits or coke. For the sake of my baby and my energy levels, fruit is staying on the menu.

Sweet dreams
Avoiding sugar for a week was not nearly as hard as I thought it would be. This is partly because:
1. It is June and the strawberries are particularly sweet right now.
2. It has been very hot and I haven't felt much like eating anything, not even cake.
3. I had the motivation of weight control spurring me on.

I had thought that tampering with food might end up having more to do with my thighs than my relationship with God, and I think that it did: pregnancy and all, I am still thinking far too much about my weight and size, and resisting sweet treats felt good, like I was back in charge of my body having let it all go temporarily. But, having said that, there is spiritual benefit to taking charge of our appetites, and it did stop me from getting comfort from calories instead of seeking it from Jesus. And it was a chance for me to talk to God about food – to repent for overeating, to ask for help in controlling my greed, to discuss with him ways to live counterculturally in a society that ascribes value judgements to dress sizes. All these issues are profoundly spiritual in the sense that to be a Christian means to see the impact of following Christ in every nook and cranny of our lives.

The 40-day Fast

I put my questions to someone who has really done this thing properly, and am seriously impressed…

Whenever the topic of fasting has come up, my mind immediately conjures up an intriguing girl I knew vaguely at university. I had arrived somewhat spiritually malnourished after spending several months misbehaving in Africa, and I wanted to grow healthy. I looked around me for inspiration, and one of the people who gave me vision for how dramatic and vivid a life lived at full pelt towards holiness could look like was Joanna. Joanna chose to begin her time at university by undertaking a 40-day fast. This was not a 40-day chocolate fast – an impressive feat in itself – but forty days without eating at all. Recently, Joanna cropped up in my life again, and I seized the opportunity to sit her down and grill her about her fast, and her general thoughts about fasting ten years on.

I had wondered whether Joanna would look back on her young self with slight condescension and bemusement. Many people are at their most extreme during university years, piercing unlikely body parts, going on marches against third world debt, debating the meaning of life over greasy brunches, and flirting with interesting ideologies and members of the opposite sex – well that is what I did at university anyway. As soon as we began to talk, however, it became clear that Joanna was a much more evolved human being at that life stage than I had been. The fast is something she still considers a high point in her spiritual journey, and had been approached with great maturity and careful thought. Before we got into the deep stuff though, I had lots of rather trivial questions to ask her about the practicalities of these forty food-free days.

Did she really not eat at all?

No food at all, other than one piece of pizza at a friend's birthday meal where she felt that God said it was more important to break the fast than cause a stir. Otherwise, she got by on various drinks, including hot chocolate and fruit juices.

How did she have the energy to study?

She was young! And she was doing a degree course with a relatively light workload.

Did she have medical supervision?

Not officially, but there are a lot of guidelines for a fast like this available, and she did read up on them. She said she was in good physical health at the time, with no history of eating disorders.

(I would want to add a cautionary note here: *if you are considering a fast of this length you should do it under proper supervision.*)

Did she find she was pleased to be losing weight and did this undermine her primary, spiritual purposes for fasting?

She had a fleeting feeling of satisfaction when she borrowed a skinny friend's jeans and they fitted, but it wasn't something that she thought about often, as weight had never been a big preoccupation for her.

Did anyone worry that she had an eating disorder and try to force her to eat?

As it was the beginning of her time at university, no one knew her well enough to notice her changing appearance. Her flatmates had very different timetables so they didn't notice her strange behaviour at mealtimes, and her family didn't know what she was up to.

I was curious to know how the fast had come about. Joanna had a strong faith in God from childhood. She said she has sometimes wished she had a more exciting story to tell, but mostly considers her long history of belonging to Christ as pure grace. As an 18-year-old, she took the step of turning down a place at Exeter University in response to a sense that God had something else in mind for her. After a year or so of working as a church youth worker, she began to wonder about what might be around the corner.

'I spent a lot of time praying about what was next, and felt God speak to me about going to Birmingham. I knew this was for the degree, and for the learning, but I also knew it was for something more. I felt like I was going with a purpose, and in response to God's leading, and so I was really keen to get God's perspective on why I was there, and really start well, and start the way I wanted to continue.'

So the fast was a means of hearing God speak about why he had wanted her to go to Birmingham?

'The heart of why I wanted to do it was to gain greater clarity. The fast was something that I felt God had invited me to do, so I had the expectation that I would hear from him. It says in Scripture that if we seek him he'll be found by us. In some ways it was as simple as saying, "I'll seek you. You're all that I long

for". And the fast was me giving a physical aspect to that – letting God know that I really meant it – I really did want to seek him, whatever the cost. You find that you don't have to take a very big step before God has taken a huge leap towards you.'

So did she hear from God about why she was at Birmingham University, I asked nosily.

'Yes. It wasn't specifically why God had brought me there, but more about discovering a deeper intimacy with God, knowing more, hearing more. There were scriptures that I discovered during that time that were written into my life. It was an agenda setting time, in the sense that I said to God, "I am here to meet with you, to know you more, to live a life that reflects you, to share more of you with other people." And that has really been the agenda of my life since then.'

For Joanna, those forty days were about a replacement of food with spiritual nourishment. She feels strongly that the meaning of a fast is far more to do with embracing prayer and the Word of God than about denying yourself calories. It was a time in which she established a strong personal discipline of prayer, went to all the prayer meetings going, and studied, memorised and listened to Scripture.

Our chat had given me food for thought, but now it was lunch time, and my stomach was rumbling. We wrapped up our chat and headed for the kitchen.

Reflections

I have to conclude that fasting has an important part to play in the nurture of a mature spiritual life. I wondered at the outset what the point of it was, and at the end of the month, here are my thoughts on the purposes or uses of fasting, whether from food or other things:

- Fasting takes us into a place of discomfort, in which we have the choice to reach out to God in true vulnerability.
- Fasting reminds us of the enforced deprivations endured by most of the world. It cannot take us even close to what this kind of suffering feels like, but it may spark our imagination and our compassion.
- Fasting takes us into a sort of silence in which we can hear both God and ourselves more clearly – once we are able to tune out our grumbling stomachs!
- Fasting is more about the goal (intimacy with God) than about the loss of things we like. In a sense, we lose what we want to gain what we need.
- Fasting is a counterbalance to the self-indulgence that our culture promotes and expects of us.
- Fasting catches our attention and clears our minds, giving us a chance to experience God more acutely, pray with greater urgency and sharpen our awareness of all things spiritual.
- Fasting shows us our addictions and allows us to challenge the hold they have over us.
- Fasting reveals sin, and can lead to a greater appreciation of grace.

This has been an interesting month, and I have learnt a lot. It has made me think that I should give food fasts a regular place in my spiritual life, despite the complications, and once my body has become my own again, I will look at how and when that should happen. In the meantime, I am drinking my morning cup of tea with a whole new level of enjoyment. Praise God from whom all blessings flow!

CHAPTER THREE

BIBLE

*Your word is a lamp to my feet
and a light for my path.*

PSALM 119:105

I was introduced to the Bible as a child. I knew all about 'Bimbam and Baby Eyes' (Abraham and Isaac), Jonah and the whale, Noah's ark and all the other Old Testament stories that were deemed suitable for children. It is amazing that I didn't have horrendous nightmares – most of these tales should have a Certificate 18. After all, Bimbam put Baby Eyes on a pile of wood ready to burn him alive, and although Noah was cosy on his big boat with his family and the animals, they were floating on a multitude of drowned bodies. The New Testament is not short on gore either – John the Baptist literally loses his head, there are demons all over the place throwing kids into fires and destroying herds of pigs, and the crucifixion accounts do not underplay the cruelty of this inhuman form of torture. It is all pretty complicated stuff. Anyway, as I was saying, this all-important book has been a part of my life since way back.

When I was about ten, I graduated to a bright yellow hard-backed Good News Bible, which I covered with religiously-themed stickers and desecrated with a highlighter, randomly selecting passages to be embellished in pink. I had picked up the idea from somewhere that people who took their faith seriously tended to have tatty, written-in Bibles. A little later I used age-appropriate Scripture Union Bible notes in sporadic fashion, and began years of battling 'missed-Quiet-Time-guilt'.

I had an encounter with the Holy Spirit when I was eleven which propelled me into the Bible with a zeal that I look back on with wonder. This is one of the reasons that I believe the experience really was a genuine meeting with God and not self-generated emotional hysteria. One of the lasting fruits of that time was the comfort that I got from biblical sources during episodes of depression at boarding school. Another was a deep conviction that I needed to use it to get my bearings – that it needed to be my true north as it were. Even when I have deliberately gone off course I have been mindful of the biblical ideals that I am straying from.

At university, I began to feel that I was approaching the difficulties I encountered in my reading of the Bible dishonestly and that I lacked the integrity to come to genuine conclusions. I was squinting at the pages trying to see them through the framework of belief I had been taught and afraid to acknowledge the big questions in case the answers undermined the foundations of my faith. But by trying to eliminate the mystery I was missing the majesty – I was squeezing the beauty out of the book and out of the great adventure of following Christ. It was at this juncture that the possibility of doing a post-graduate theology course came up. I had left a serious relationship and my future was an empty slate. I headed off for Vancouver, British Columbia to study at Regent College. Over the next four years I realised with growing amazement just how complicated and profound and inspired this ancient compilation of documents really is. I acquired a toolkit to handle it with greater confidence, and I learnt that in and through its very human origins, God has revealed his character, his thoughts and his plans. I marvel now that I had the opportunity to sit around at the feet of wise teachers, with the time for reading and coffee drinking and discussion and prayer. I am not sure I knew what a luxurious existence that was – I probably moaned about deadlines.

While living in Canada I met Shawn and we got married. In our first year of marriage we started every day with a cup of tea in bed, and a time reading the Bible and praying together. I was cohabiting with my old friend depression once again, and this routine was a lifeline to me. Depression always affects the way I read the Bible. I identify with the 'wicked' whenever 'the wicked' are mentioned, as in Proverbs 10:20: 'The tongue of the righteous is choice silver, but the heart of the wicked is of little value.' I hear all the judgement and miss the mercy and grace. I get overwhelmed by the culturally obscure references, and take on the pain of the difficult stories. Have you ever read the account of the Israelite judge, Jephthah, having to sacrifice his beloved daughter because of a foolish vow he made to God (Judges 11) when you are feeling emotionally fragile? Reading the Bible with Shawn helped me to hear God speaking gently to me through his Word. We would chew over the implications of what we'd read together, and he'd help me understand passages in light of the whole Bible, because he seemed to have most of it memorised.

When we moved to England a year and a half later I began working at a leading national medical charity as a support worker, and wrote my first book in my spare time. I had spent the last four years cocooned in the company of fellow Christians, and my work context was a chance to test my biblical convictions and strength of character. The challenges were numerous – would I be able to behave with integrity when my workmates were all filling in timesheets dishonestly and even my boss encouraged me to do the same? Would I show patience and love to a resident who was verbally and physically abusive to me? Would I be able to have an attitude of contentment when I was bored, stressed, and demoralised? How would I hold on to my understanding of God's goodness when caring for people whose bodies were regularly thrown to the ground with violent convulsions, and who had been born with damaged brains and deformed limbs? The answer to those questions is: sometimes. I grappled with myself and with God and with this wonderful and maddening book and occasionally I did the right thing.

In my first year of motherhood I found it very hard to incorporate regular Bible reading into my life. For a few months it happened at church and with my small group and that's about the extent of it. I have to say, I did notice a difference in myself – I gave in to self-pity more easily, I was preoccupied with the details of my own life and I felt spiritually listless. I think I really need the input of the Word of God in a fundamental way. Nick Spenser and Graham Tomlin say this:

'We read Scripture day after day, to become familiar with it, to fill our minds with it, to memorise it, so that it frequently comes to mind as we interact with people, books, art and opinions. In fact there is little chance of…any kind of Christian maturity without a regular habit of reading a section of the Bible just about every day.'[1]

In the last few months I have been trying to follow a program that takes you through the Bible in a year, by giving you a daily dose of Old and New Testament, and a Psalm or a Chapter of Proverbs. It is a little fragmented but a more balanced diet than you would get starting at page one and working through to the back cover. I usually read it when Alexa is eating her cereal, so I don't give it as much attention as it deserves, and I certainly haven't managed to do it every day. I am looking forward to trying out some different ways of getting my Bible-fix this month.

Jo's Doctrine of the Bible

Before I begin, I thought I would put together a statement about what I believe about the Bible and the place it has in my life. Have you ever considered doing this yourself? I think it could be a helpful exercise.

– I believe that the Bible, in its entirety, is the revealed Word of God.

- I therefore submit myself to its authority, as far as both my understanding of it and my wilful nature allows.
- I believe that God chose to reveal himself in and through humankind, in particular cultures and at particular times, and therefore that there is serious work to be done in order to understand what it was he had to say to people at the time and for us who hear it today. Issues of translation, manuscript age, condition, consistency, and the evolvement of the canon don't scare me, but I do acknowledge their existence.
- I believe that the Bible contains many different genres and that we need to pay attention to the kind of literature we are reading if we are to hear what it is saying. A shopping list is not a poem, a short story is not a historical account, and a bank statement is not a love letter.
- I believe that through reading the Bible we can get to know God and that in knowing God we can become increasingly like him. Knowing God and growing in love for him, for others and for his creation is for me why reading the Bible is an essential part of the spiritual life.

Week One

Meditating

As usual, I am beginning this month with a great sense of inadequacy – who am I to be writing on matters spiritual? I am a pilgrim, along with all who want to know Christ, but my pilgrimage is meandering and slow. If I was on the motorway I would be the annoying Sunday driver causing a tailback by drifting between lanes at 55 mph, the windows down, the map flapping dangerously around on the dashboard, and the music too loud for me to concentrate. When I think about people who meditate on Scripture, they are very different people from me – holier, calmer and more centred. I feel that before I can even open the Bible to begin this task, I ought to read lots of monastic literature with contemporary study guides. That said, my purpose here is to demonstrate that we can all begin somewhere, and that you don't need to be particularly impressive to adopt any of the spiritual practices out there. So Meditation 101 here we come. Week one of the Bible month is going to be spent in the company of four verses. This way of approaching the Bible is known as *Lectio Divina* and there are four elements involved:

1. Reading with a listening spirit
2. Reflecting on what we hear
3. Praying in response
4. Contemplating what we will do with what we've heard – how we will obey it.

Seven days with four Verses

I can't say there was anything particularly profound about the way I chose which bit of the Bible to spend this week with. I have one of those editions that has the words of Jesus in red, and I thought it would be nice to listen to Jesus in the first person, so I ended up with John 14:1–4. OK, I know it is more complicated than that – his words are recorded by someone else, in a language that was then translated and translated again and copied by hand and then copied again etc. And anyway, ALL Scripture is God-breathed, not just the bits in red print. Please forgive my over-simplification.

This passage comes part way through the Last Supper. Jesus and his closest friends are sharing the Passover meal in a private room, and talking late into the night. Every word he says is burnt into the minds of those present, haunting them long after the events of the following days have played out.

I begin my reading by trying to imagine myself into the room. Perhaps the floor has terracotta tiles, and the walls are whitewashed. I picture it a little like some of the houses I knew growing up in Portugal – built for the heat, with cool stone walls and deep set, narrow windows. It is lit by oil lamps which smoke and sputter and surround themselves with warm pools of light. Where the lamps' domain ends, the darkness is deep. The remains of the meal cover the low table: the roast lamb, the half-drunk cups of wine. The flat bread is still being picked at. The heat of the day lingers but the night is bringing with it a fragrant cool.

I try to capture the dread and fear that must have intruded into this atmosphere of quiet celebration, as Jesus tries to help them understand what is about to happen – that he must leave them. Everyone in the room by this point, Judas having just left, loves him completely and has abandoned life as they knew it to follow him around the countryside, soaking up everything he has to teach them. They have experienced his physical presence day in day out. They trust him and depend on him, and they are now being told, 'I will be with you only a little longer. You will look for me, and just as I told the Jews, so I tell you now: Where I am going, you cannot come' (John 13:33).

And then I try to hear him say to me, as he said to them on that night, the night before his brutal torture and death: 'Do not let your hearts be troubled. Trust in God; trust also in me. My Father's house has plenty of room; if that were not so, would I have told you that I am going there to prepare a place for you? And if I go and prepare a place for you, I will come back and take you to be with me that you also may be where I am. You know the way to the place where I am going' (John 14:1–4).

Let me pull you away from that room and those people, and land you in the more prosaic world of my life. Those words of Jesus have been speaking to me this week in the following situations and events. I was on craft duty at my toddler group. I had my parents to stay for the night, and my recently bereaved uncle came for an afternoon visit. Wimbledon was in its final stages. I had a midwife appointment, a visit from one of the church teenagers and a youth weekend away. I took Alexa swimming at a friend's pool three times – the weather has been sweltering. I went food shopping. I went to Heathrow Airport to meet up with my adopted godmother and my Canadian psychiatrist who were in transit for a couple of hours. I spent time praying with a friend whose best friend from childhood died suddenly in November. I met with my prayer triplet. I ate an entire bar of Cadbury's Fruit and Nut in just under two days (we're talking a BIG bar) and it made me feel awful. I started trying to make plans for the three weeks that Shawn is gone this summer, and realised I have three talks to prepare and an article to write in the next three weeks. I didn't do anything constructive about that realisation.

Although I randomly selected what to read, Jesus' words in John's Gospel have seemed to speak directly to me at each turn. I have heard him say to me, 'You can choose to trust me. Don't let your heart be troubled. Remember the home that is waiting for you in my Father's house.' This is comfort for Amanda as she grieves her friend, and my uncle, as he begins life without his wife. And it gives a longer perspective to my short-term worries about getting my talks ready in time, how I will cope with two children and being crazy-newborn-tired again, whether I will be OK on my own for so much of August.

I really feel as though I have appropriated the Passover supper with Jesus, as though it is now one of my own memories. Jesus spoke these words. He had his feet on this very planet. He is alive and with me now, and I am getting to know him through these first-hand accounts that I am blessed to have access to. Reading in this way has been a rich experience, and if I have inspired you to try it, I don't think you will be disappointed.

Week Two

Studying
Studying the Bible is a whole different approach, but just as exciting in my opinion. This week I am going to gear my brain up, and read the Bible as a student, paying attention to context, content, language and

authorial intent, using commentaries, concordances and different translations. This should not be an interruption of my devotional journey into the Bible, but an enhancement of it. As Eugene Peterson says:

'…without exegesis, spirituality gets sappy, soupy. Spirituality without exegesis becomes self-indulgent. Without disciplined exegesis spirituality develops into an idiolect in which I define all the key verbs and nouns out of my own experience. And prayer ends up limping along in sighs and stutters.'[2]

The first thing I did this week was to read the whole letter of 1 Timothy through in a sitting. I then summarised it chunk by chunk, trying to follow the flow of logic and understand why each bit followed on from the last. The letter seems to have some major concerns, namely how Timothy should handle false teachers in the Ephesian church, some guidelines for the appointment, qualities and conduct of church leaders, a godly attitude to wealth, the church's responsibility towards widows and the role of women in the congregation. How these concerns are ordered in the letter seemed to me to be a bit random, as though Paul's thoughts were coming thick and fast and he was plucking them from the air as they flew past. (You can actually catch birds like this. My friend Colin once pulled a seagull out of the sky by its leg, to both of their great surprise). Fortunately, the *Bible Background Commentary*[3] was able to offer a feasible explanation – the haphazard nature of the missive has a precedent in Hellenistic royal correspondence ('*mandata principis*'), in which a ruler would issue disjointed directives to delegates governing distant provinces.

As I went through the letter I noted down the bits that I didn't understand, with the intention of sorting out my confusion later in the week. I didn't know what to make of Paul's statement that 'women will be saved through childbearing' (1 Timothy 2:15), or whether the rule that only those with well-behaved children should be church leaders ought to be applied today (we all know that pastors' kids are very likely to have green streaks in their hair and cigarettes in their back pockets – are these things grounds for their parents' dismissal?), or what it means that younger widows who have remarried have broken their first pledge (5:12). I hoped that some background reading might shed some light on these puzzles.

Before beginning each study session, I tried to get into a prayerful, listening mindset. I can see that this way of reading the Bible could easily become just an academic exercise, but also that it could be a very powerful way of digesting the Word of God. There was a big difference in the impact it had on me depending on my attitude as I approached these times. On a couple of evenings I was less inclined to engage my whole self, and found it a bit dry and even tedious. But on other days it completely captured me, heart and soul, and I found myself chewing over what I had learnt and wanting to absorb it and understand it at the deepest level.

There are many different study aids you can use if you decide to spend some study time with the Bible. I highly recommend that you begin by getting hold of a copy of *How to Read the Bible for All Its Worth: a Guide to Understanding the Bible* by Gordon D. Fee and Douglas Stuart.[4] It gives pointers for reading each of the different genres found in the Bible, and while content-heavy and fairly meaty, is also very accessible. Then there are all sorts of different commentaries and dictionaries and study guides you can use, lots of which are available on computer software which saves bookshelf space. This week as well as the *Bible Background Commentary*, I used *The Bible Knowledge Commentary*[5] and the *Life Application Bible Study*[6] on 1 Timothy. These gave me a good spectrum of information and came from varied theological standpoints so I could see what the different views on each point were and try to come to my own opinion. I am still confused about widows' pledges but I know what I think about being saved by childbirth now.

You will have to do your own research on that one, or we'd end up with a book within a book here!

Week Three

Reading in community

Reading the Bible alone is a relatively new pursuit. For centuries it was read exclusively in a communal setting, and while we have all gained a lot from having individual access to God's Word, we have also lost some benefits that came from hearing it as a group. Much of the Bible was addressed to a collective audience. When we read 'you' we tend to assume it refers to 'me', whereas it is actually to 'us'. The lack of a second person plural in the English language really lets us down here. If we are studying the Bible together we might be more able to hear it less individualistically. We will also benefit from the insights of others and perhaps come to discover meanings in the text that we might have missed.

The Bible usually features prominently when Christians get together to worship God. In many Churches, a passage will be read aloud and then someone will speak about it, having spent significant time trying to grasp what it has to say. In this way we benefit from the work and expertise of our leaders, we are given the opportunity to hear God's Word as a group (of course we can sit there and not listen. You can take a horse to water…) and we might gain some insight that will change us for the better. You might be able to skim over a challenge when you are reading in the privacy of your bedroom, but it is harder to avoid when it is the subject of a half-hour sermon. I am privileged to be a member of a church that has a very gifted preaching team, and when I am receptive to hearing God speak, he always speaks through the biblical preaching I receive week in week out.

Alexa always has a Bible story before bed. Last night we read the story of The Good Samaritan. She wanted to know if robbers live up trees, and if they do, whether they fall out when they go to sleep. I find it interesting what aspect of a story she will grab onto – it is never the obvious theme. She has been learning about Noah's ark at church, and as far as I can tell, the only enduring lesson she has learnt is that rainbows are found when there is rain and sunshine at the same time. I overheard her talking about this story with my friend's son in the car the other day. He said that we need to forgive Jesus for the flood. 'That wasn't Jesus. That was God!' his sister chipped in. Children are very good at getting us to wrestle with the awkwardness in the biblical narratives, and I am looking forward to having more and more family discussions as the girls grow up. It is a great comfort to know that their father is so clued-up on the subject though!

On Thursday mornings I meet with a group of women for Bible study and prayer. We are looking at the gospel of Mark at the moment. I have always considered Mark my least favourite Gospel, something to do with the fact that I studied it for GCSE (UK school exam), but I am growing to love it again as I look at it more closely in the company of my friends. It is not that I am finding new bits – every word was pored over by my 15-year-old self – more that it is catching my imagination and it is helping me get to know Jesus. Well-led Bible studies are a joy to participate in. We all know that they are not always well led, and there is nothing quite as dispiriting as a bad Bible study. How painful is it to sit waiting to see who will answer the latest mind-bogglingly bland question? 'What is Jesus saying here?' Everyone studies their open Bibles – could it be that there is a hidden depth to be mined? It couldn't really be this obvious could it? Silence. Then someone bravely volunteers what can only be the right answer: 'Jesus is saying they should go over to the other side of the lake.' Thoughtful 'hmmmm' from the leader. As I was saying, my Thursday Bible study is nothing at all like this. If yours is, at least you are spending some time with the Good Book, even if it is full of annoying interruptions.

Week Four

Memorising

When I was a child my greatest fear was of being kidnapped. I am sure
this is because we had a banner in our church that said 'Remember
Terry Waite' and it had been explained to me that this man, Terry, had
been kidnapped and had been held hostage for what seemed from my
perspective to have been an endless amount of time. I am sure that
it seemed like a long time to Terry too. I assumed that one day I too
would be kept in solitary captivity, and I strategised about how I would
occupy myself. I planned to do star jumps, make up stories, think about
my friends and family one by one and scratch pictures into the floor. As
I grew up, I began to think it would be a good idea to have chunks of the
Bible memorised so that I would be more able to hold onto my faith as I
sat there alone in the dark. This is perhaps a slightly strange and morbid
motivation for committing chunks of scripture to memory, but I suppose
the benefits would be the same in less extreme circumstances too. If our
minds are seeped in the Word of God then we will be able to draw on it
wherever we are and its wisdom will be at hand whenever we need it.

Like most people, I have a good memory for some things and a goldfish
memory for other things. Goldfish supposedly hold things in mind for
around three seconds, hence they can swim around a small bowl of
water being endlessly surprised by the view. My most shameful memory
lapse is celebrating Shawn's birthday on the wrong day three years
running, fortunately two days early and not two days late, and I still
have no idea what my mobile phone number is. But even those of us
with fish brains can find ways of hiding God's Word in our hearts (Psalm
119:11). Here are some ideas:

1. Write verses on sticky notes and stick them in places you often visit. A
   good place for me would be the fridge, and perhaps a good verse for
   the fridge would be Galatians 5:16: 'Walk by the Spirit, and you will

not gratify the desires of the sinful nature.' My sinful nature desires naughty things from the fridge.

2. A lot of worship songs have lyrics lifted straight from the Bible. Matt Redman, a singer and song writer, says that one of the benefits of writing worship songs is that you can plagiarise the Bible and instead of getting sued you are applauded for your excellent content.[7] When the Bible is set to music it is very easy to remember.

3. Resolve to commit a certain amount of scripture to memory and then do it. You could find someone else to do it with and test each other periodically.

As we consider the challenge of memorising a few verses, we can be spurred on by the example of many Orthodox Jews who from the age of twelve have often learnt the entire Torah by heart – that is the first five books of the Bible. What better use could we put our minds to than filling them with the stories of God's revelation to his creation?

A mind like a sieve can still hold big chunks
I loved spending time with Hebrews 11 and 12 last week, and so I decided to try and memorise all 29 verses of Hebrews 12. I did it by reading the whole chapter every day and adding a paragraph on to the ones I had already learnt. I found it was helpful to say it out loud.

Once in mind, it began to get absorbed and digested and integrated into my thoughts and from there into my life. Having this chapter to hand at all times meant that rather than paying fifteen minutes of attention to God's Word and then going on my way, I found myself mulling it over, or discovering that it offered me a new approach to a difficulty, or realising that I could offer its wisdom to a friend in the course of a conversation. This was a really good and worthwhile thing to do, and I enthusiastically recommend it.

The Wright Man for the Job:

Finding an available hour in Chris Wright's schedule is not entirely straightforward so I considered myself very fortunate when we met at Lord's Restaurant in central London for a curry buffet earlier this week. Chris is the International Director of Langham Partnership International, a charity involved in resourcing preachers and teachers of theology in the Majority World. He is also a prolific author, an Old Testament scholar with a particular interest in ethics and mission, a member of the ministry team at All Souls Church in London and chairman of the Theology Working Group for the Lausanne Movement 2010.

I wanted to know how important he felt it was to read the Bible, and whether he considered the traditional 'Quiet Time' model a valid way of doing so. I began by asking him what his current Bible reading habits looked like – did he have a Quiet Time? Chris was raised in Northern Ireland by Christian parents who encouraged him to adopt a discipline of daily Bible reading which he continued until early adulthood. He admitted that although he would still consider this to be an ideal, he couldn't truthfully say that he now has a daily Quiet Time in the traditional sense. All this early Bible reading, though, has stood him in good stead; the Bible is so deeply embedded in his consciousness that he now thinks *with* it rather than *about* it. Before I can even wonder if he has just confessed to being a lapsed Bible-reader, he clarifies:

'I would never say that learning the Bible as a child means I no longer have need to read it now. The times I do set aside to study and read the Bible are very precious to me. In fact I find myself experiencing a frisson of expectancy and anticipation whenever I sit down to read it. I always have a sense of wondering what I will find that I haven't seen before, because it is the living Word of God to me. It still has power. It still speaks.'

And he sets aside plenty of time, not least because his job involves speaking and writing about the Bible.

I wanted to continue exploring the Quiet Time idea, and I wondered out loud whether this practice of reading short sections of scripture, by yourself, on a daily basis might have contributed to the current tendency among Evangelical Christians to relate to God in an individualistic and egocentric manner, always seeking to discover what God is saying to *me*, about his plan for *my* life. Chris concedes that it may feed into that inclination, but his sense is that the more self-absorbed Christians probably aren't reading the Bible much in the first place, a far greater danger to his mind.

'My fear for a generation who might have, in a pendulum swing away from what could have become a very legalistic, guilt-inducing quiet time routine, gone in the opposite direction and are saying I can take it or leave it, is that they will end up making up their own religion. You are not actually functioning as a disciple of Jesus, who said "learn of me", if you are not reading the Bible, because the only place you can learn of Jesus is in the Scriptures, both Old and New Testament. I would urge people always to get back to the Bible whatever way they choose to do it, whether every so often setting aside a good amount of time to really study, or getting into a Bible study group.'

It seems ironic to me that in a time and place where the Bible is readily available, there are those of us who don't value it enough to prioritise reading it on a daily basis. Chris agrees:

'The fact is that we now have more Bibles than ever in the English language and publishers are falling over themselves to publish Boys' Bibles and Girls' Bibles and so on, and yet it seems the more Bibles there are the less people are reading it. In some parts of the world where Bibles are actually still scarce, people value it hugely. I know someone from the Democratic Republic of

Congo who said that in his younger years, if anyone in his family was lucky enough to get a Bible, they would literally cut it into pieces to spread it around.'

I think ruefully of the seven or eight Bibles lying around at home, different translations, sizes and colours, and none of them opened nearly enough.

It is pretty clear that Chris thinks people should be reading the Bible. My next line of enquiry is whether he thinks it is dangerous to read the Bible with no background knowledge or help.

'It is potentially dangerous if people treat the Bible as a magic book – "I'll just find the verse for me today". If you only read small chunks you never see the total picture – you never get the sense of where that Bible verse fits in the whole picture, looking forwards, looking backwards; you are not placing the text in its proper context. But I wouldn't want to suggest that new believers or enquirers can't read the Bible without commentaries or great works of theology to assist them. You don't have to be an expert in order for God to speak to you through the Bible. It would be a form of arrogance to believe that. A classic fault of pharasaism was the belief that ordinary people couldn't be trusted to really know the Bible for themselves. However it would also be arrogant to think that you can just pick up the Bible and figure out what it says by yourself without asking anybody for help. Some people would spiritualise that and say that the Holy Spirit will teach you, that the Bible is self-sufficient. In some sense it is – it is the full revelation of God, but we need to be humble enough to get help from the scholars who have studied the history and know the background.'

Is there a difference between 'scholarly' and 'devotional' Bible reading, or must they always coexist?

'I believe that there is a place for both the scholarly and the devotional use of the Bible. I handle the Bible professionally as a teacher and I love doing that. There is nothing I love more than getting into a passage and working on it in order to preach it or teach it. But there have been times in my life when I have been under severe pressure, emotionally or morally, and have been in a mess with God and I have found in those times that the Bible can speak very directly, straight off the page in ways that make my scholarly head protest, "This wasn't written to you!" Yet my heart tells me that it is being spoken to me, into my soul, to convict, to correct, to comfort – and I get a sense that God is saying, "It's OK – I'm still here. I'm in control."'

Reflections

It seems to me that the message Chris would like to put across is that however we absorb God's Word, if we are to thrive and bear fruit as Christians, like the tree by the river in Psalm 1, we must have our roots dug into this book. This might be done by beginning each day with a ten minute Quiet Time. It might be done by seizing the opportunity to read whole books that you realise you haven't read in a while. You might listen to an audio Bible while you drive, attend a weekly Bible study, take a week-long summer school course at a Bible college, follow a Bible in a year reading programme, keep a Bible handy in your briefcase or handbag to read in the waiting room at the dentist, or stick verses up on sticky notes on the bathroom mirror. However it is done, it is essential to our spiritual lives that we know these scriptures inside out, so that we begin to think, act and live out of their influence.

CHAPTER FOUR:

WORSHIP

Sing to the Lord, all the earth;
*   proclaim his salvation day after day.*
Declare his glory among the nations,
*   his marvellous deeds among all peoples.*
For great is the Lord and most worthy of praise;
*   he is to be feared above all gods.*
For all the gods of the nations are idols,
*   but the Lord made the heavens…*
…Worship the Lord in the splendour of his holiness.

1 CHRONICLES 16:23–26,29

This passage seems to encapsulate much of what I understand worship to be about. Worship involves joining our voices with 'all the earth', singing, proclaiming and declaring God's salvation, his glory and his deeds to everyone who will listen, and to the Lord himself. It is something that we must do 'day after day', and that we do with a certain trepidation and respect, for 'he is to be feared'. And yet we are welcomed into the 'splendour of his holiness' and we can worship intimately in his presence.

Worship is a serious business. Before Jesus came and changed how things were done, you had to get it right or you might well die. The holiness of God was fearsome and unapproachable and gloriously terrible. The writer of the letter to the Hebrews reminds them of just how different things are under the new covenant:

You have not come to a mountain that can be touched and that is burning with fire; to darkness, gloom and storm; to a trumpet blast or to such a voice speaking words that those who heard it begged that no further word be spoken to them, because they could not bear what was commanded: If even an animal touches the mountain, it must be stoned to death. The sight was so terrifying that Moses said, 'I am trembling with fear.' (Hebrews 12:18–21)

He goes on to explain that now we have come to God made perfect by the blood of Jesus, joining the joyful assembly of angels and the church of the firstborn. But are we perhaps in danger of taking this welcome, this new freedom and graciousness too lightly? Do we take the unshakeable kingdom for granted?

Since we are receiving a kingdom that cannot be shaken, let us be thankful, and so worship God acceptably with reverence and awe, for our 'God is a consuming fire.' (Hebrews 12:28,29)

I approached this discipline knowing that worship is more than singing, but struggling to pin down an exact definition to set me off in the right direction for the month's task. After chewing it over for a while and gathering some opinions, I have settled on the following starting point: 'to consciously and exclusively acknowledge God's worth.'

It is vital that our lives are oriented around a growing knowledge and proclamation of God's worth, because the temptations towards idol worship are no less than when the people of Israel were wandering around the desert making golden calves. These days we are just as likely to worship – to consciously, if not exclusively, acknowledge the worth of – material possessions, achievement, our children, food, sex, entertainment, physical well being, youth, and a whole plethora of other lovely things that are not God and don't deserve the adoration we give them. Focusing on God's worth not only counteracts idolatry, but, as some would argue, is our primary purpose in life. Put simply, we were made to worship God.

While pagan worship is often a way of provoking a certain response from a god – perhaps the gift of rain or fertility or wealth – worship of Yahweh is a response to his initiative in our relationship. It is an expression of gratitude for his character and his actions. We have a God who is deeply and utterly mysterious and yet who has chosen to reveal himself to us, through his creation, through his prophets, through his interventions in history and ultimately by becoming incarnate and spending 33 years living among us as a divine human. We have a written record of his sayings and doings in the Bible, we live in a world that he made, and we have the Holy Spirit within us. There is really no limit to how well we can get to know this God, other than the limits of our own sinfulness and fear. In coming to know God, we are drawn to worship him: it is the only rational response.

When I was doing my masters, I was required to take a class in a discipline known as systematic theology. My professor was the world-revered J I Packer, a godly and extremely brainy theologian. He began every class by leading us in a hymn: 'Praise God from whom all blessings flow! Praise him all creatures here below. Praise him above ye heavenly host. Praise Father, Son and Holy Ghost!' He was insistent that we remember that theology should lead to doxology; in other words, as we learn about God, that knowledge ought rightly to lead us to worship him. The goal was impressive, even if I was usually more fidgety and irritable than worshipful by the end of the three-hour lecture. Even information about God can be hard to take in during siesta time, and unfortunately the class began at 2pm. The spirit is willing but the flesh in the early afternoon is oh, so weak!

So worship is consciously acknowledging God's worth, and God's worth is something he has revealed to us. The question is how to do this acknowledging. There are lots of ways I could go about exploring worship, but I am going to stay pretty simple, and look at just two categories – individual worship and corporate worship. And under those two headings, here is what I learned during the month of August.

The 'I' in Worship
(Individual Worship)

What I mean by individual worship here is the worship that happens outside of gatherings of believers for that purpose. I spent this month trying to become a generally more God-worshipping person.

Life as worship

We can express love and devotion to God through the thoughts we dwell on and the ones we summarily evict, the way we treat the people around us, the choices we make when no one is watching, and the attitude of our hearts towards him; there are many ways we can demonstrate that we want God to be glorified by our lives. Turning the whole of life into an act of worship is something that very few of us accomplish, but it is something we can all aim for.

Each summer for the past few years, Shawn and I have taken a group of teenagers from church to a Christian youth festival called Soul Survivor. There are seminars, cafes, a skating rink, gigs, art studios and all sorts of other youth-friendly venues and attractions. Main meetings happen twice daily in a tent that can hold over 10,000 people, and this is a time and place where sung worship is given priority. It is a very powerful thing to be a part of, and can be transformative for the kids we take for the week, as well as for the leaders with them. It is also not an ideal venue for a busy toddler who can't stand loud noises. This year, I found myself resentfully excluded and started to think that Alexa was preventing me from worshipping God – that is, until I had a moment of revelation. As I walked with my little daughter around the outside of the big top, played with her in the mud, fed her little bits of sandwich and kept her safe from the stampede as the meetings ended, I could worship as fully as the ecstatic singers in the midst of the action.

The potential for worship exists in everything we do. If Brother Lawrence could make dirty pot scrubbing an act of worship,[1] then I could make childcare worshipful. I don't think this means that I need to sing along to nappy changes, or create liturgies for tantrums, more that I must be the most loving and selfless mother that I can be, and mindfully dedicate my efforts to God. This is not something that comes naturally to me, and I will be working on it for longer than a month. But I am inspired to transform more of my life into God-pleasing worship. Are there things in your life that have the potential to become worship? How can you worship God as you meet with clients at work? How about during those dreadful migraines? Or as you walk your dog, do your weekly food shop, answer the phone, or take your kids to yet another after-school activity?

Reorientation

I can sometimes get things the wrong way round, and start seeing God as a character in the epic drama that is my life. While we, his human creations who bear his image, play a special and significant role in the Great Story, we shouldn't forget that he is both the star and the author. I don't need to spend long contemplating the Trinity to have any misapprehensions about the centrality of God straightened out. In worship, I decrease and he increases, and that is totally how it should be.

There are lots of things that stop us from giving God the attention and praise that he deserves – sinfulness, distractions, fatigue and so on – but one of them for me is as simple as neglecting to spend time with him, going about my day without awareness of his presence and losing the intimacy of an ongoing friendship. One way of being worshipful is as basic as giving God our focused attention. There was some overlap here

with my earlier attempts at continuous prayer, and it was good to have
another shot at this discipline.

What Are You Like?

I also spent time trying to gain a deeper understanding of God's character.
I took broad attributes such as the fact that he is loving, and tried to burrow
into what that actually means, and how I personally have experienced it.
Thinking about God's love led me to think about his patience with me, his
discipline, his presence with me in my depression, his provision of friends,
finances and direction at key moments, his willingness to have relationships
with everyone he's made despite the fact that there are so many of us –
and there was so much more to explore. Another thing I found helpful in
developing a fuller picture of God's character was to pull out descriptions
of him from the Psalms. Psalm 86, as just one example, is packed full of
the things about God that David found to be true: that God is forgiving,
good, abounding in love, faithful, compassionate, gracious, slow to anger,
merciful, and comforting.

Worshipping in the Beauty of Nature

In the middle of the month I had two weeks holiday in Wales with
my extended family. We stayed in a grey, stone cottage up a small
mountain with views of the stunning coastline – at least when the fog
lifted, which now and again it did. We had walks and beach trips and
blackberry-picking expeditions, took time to see sunsets through their
entire performances, and star-gazed on the occasional cloud-free night.
All this raw beauty truly did cause me to worship:

*'The heavens declare the glory of God; the skies proclaim the work of
his hands. Day after day they pour forth speech; night after night they
display knowledge.'* (Psalm 19:1,2)

When I think of the times I have worshipped God most wholeheartedly,
spontaneously, and authentically, they have usually been outdoors,

in places of natural beauty: Galiano Island in British Columbia, a pine forest overlooking an estuary in southern Portugal, and in a dramatic summer thunderstorm in France. Creation tells us so much about the creator. Is there anywhere beautiful where you find you feel especially close to God? Do you sense yourself being prompted to praise him when you are confronted by a breathtaking view?

Singing Solo (with the backing of Ms Scott)
The journey home from Wales had some interesting moments. Shawn had left a few days before on a mini-sabbatical and so I had to do the five-hour drive myself. I am not very confident behind the wheel and I was dreading the trip, but I had a new worship album and had planned to use the time to sing along and then have an experience to write about (this book has definitely been good motivation to be more spiritually inclined than I might otherwise be!). This was working out OK to begin with, but then Alexa began to object strongly from the back seat: 'Mummy, don't sing with the lady. Don't sing. STOP SINGING MUMMY!' It wasn't worth winding my daughter up, so I let the lady sing on without me.

It was to the soundtrack of Kathryn Scott's heavenly voice that our near-death motorway incident occurred. A large chunk of wood, possibly a railway sleeper according to the man who assessed the damage to all four wheels later, fell from a truck into our lane. There was no time to slow down or make any kind of decision about how to deal with the obstacle, we just rammed into it, breaking it into pieces, and watching it fly out behind us into the cars behind. Amazingly, that was the height of the drama. No one crashed, no one was hurt. Even our car was deemed fit to take us the rest of the way home – another hour's drive – after receiving some first aid at a friendly garage just off the motorway. The trauma I experienced was largely to do with the vulnerability of being in charge of a 2-year-old and a very large bump. Having listened to my album for three hours on repeat, I had the songs circling around my mind throughout the ordeal and the words reminded me of God's presence, goodness, sovereignty and comfort.

The tongues of angels

During this month I also took out and dusted off a gift that God gave me when I was 11 and which was at one time something that I used to worship him a lot. Somewhere along the way it got shelved, and I want to rediscover it. I am referring to the gift of speaking in tongues. I first encountered this spiritual gift on a beach trip with some students who had been staying with my family on their way to a big charismatic conference in Lisbon. They took me under their wing and I was delighted to be singled out and given attention. On this particular afternoon two of them, Helen and Pete needed some couple time and had wandered off along the shoreline, leaving me under the beach umbrella with Pippa. By the time they returned it was to find that I had been knocked out by the Holy Spirit with such force that I could barely move.

I remember that the golden late afternoon sun on my skin felt like an embrace from God. I could not stop laughing and crying, and somewhere along the way I had begun to say words that were neither English nor Portuguese. Later I would spend hours researching this phenomenon, trying to understand what its purpose was, how I should use it, whether it was genuine or valid or really from God. A good place to start if you are also curious is 1 Corinthians chapters 12, 13 and 14. But even before I had the most rudimentary understanding of this strange gift, it had enabled me to praise God in a new way. This is a deeply personal way of communicating with God, and something that belongs in private worship, unless a person feels compelled to speak it out and it is followed by an interpretation. I think as a gift it is intended to be used quietly, to enable our worship to continue when words fail. As Paul writes: '...those who speak in a tongue do not speak to other people but to God. Indeed, no one understands them; they utter mysteries by the Spirit' (1 Corinthians 14:3). I regret that I have neglected to worship

God using this language he gave me and it has been a pleasure to rediscover it.

All Together Now
(Corporate Worship)

While we can and should worship God at all times and in all places, there is something particularly right and good about worshipping with other Christians. We come together because it is together that we are the bride of Christ, because we need each other's sharp edges to smooth us into holiness, and because when we look God-wards together our individualism is transcended and we unite under the authority of our common father. More than this, community and relationality is modelled for us by the Trinity. In an article for the journal *Crux*, Julie Canlis argues that:

'A trinitarian spirituality de facto cannot be a spirituality without the senses, the body, nature, art or that great body – the church. When we became Christians, we did not do so by virtue of our new knowledge, but by virtue of our new relationships. Through baptism "in the name of the Father, of the Son, and of the Holy Spirit" the Spirit leads believers simultaneously into a communion both trinitarian and ecclesial. Every time we go to church, we declare that we are not individuals – as the culture around us would have us believe – but rather are made up of these new relations.'[2]

Whether these relationships can be carried out virtually is a live debate. Today we can be part of a church and never come face to face with a single other person. A few examples of web churches are www.stpixels.com, www.churchoffools.com and online-churches.net, where you can join in a 'live' streamed service at any time of day or night. My own thinking on this is tending towards the conclusion that, if at all possible, we probably need to gather together in actual time and physical space, but feel free to argue with me – you could send me an email if you like!

Jesus worshipped communally. He grew up attending his local synagogue, but also making an annual pilgrimage to Jerusalem with his family for Passover (Luke 2:41,42). We live now in an era when God's temple is no longer a building but a people. But there is still something very powerful and significant when we have the opportunity to gather en masse in worship. My church goes every summer to a festival called New Wine at which around 12,000 Christians spend a week camping and worshipping God together. My friend Ally says it feels like an annual pilgrimage, a key part of her own spiritual journey, that of her family, and that of the church. This year it rained incessantly, churning the fields into wallowy mud and threatening to discourage the most cheery delegates. But it was still, according to Ally, a highlight of the year. I dropped in for a day and here are some of my thoughts and observations:

– When we sing to God with thousands of others, it is easy to picture the angels swooping with joy through the air above our heads and the Father, Son and Holy Spirit enjoying our company and smiling on our enthusiasm.

– I found myself wondering what was generating the electricity. Was it the hype, the emotional tones of the singers, the low lighting or the feeling of being a part of something much bigger than myself or my local church? Perhaps it doesn't matter. If this setting releases us to worship God with our emotions as well as our minds then I think that is good. If the low lighting allows us to lose some inhibition and focus on God, not on what people may think of us, great. If we are caught up in a sense of being a part of something bigger than us, then that sense is just a glimpse of reality. We are a part of something bigger than us.

I don't have a great track record of seeking out churches to go to when on holiday. I tend to have a holiday from church attendance as well as from other aspects of regular life. While in Wales this summer I did go on one of the two Sundays, mostly so I could write about it. I'm not very holy am I? The village church has a lot of significance for our family: my parents were married there, so was one of my sisters, and my grandfather is buried in the churchyard. In the Sunday services I have attended over the years I have more often found myself gathering material for comic anecdotes than communing with God and fellow Christians. It is easier for me to mock and clock-watch than truly engage in worship when the style, content and format are all at odds with my natural preferences. I am not proud to admit that, as it reveals a lot about my immaturity, and shows I have some basic misconceptions about worship. If I really understood that worship is about declaring the worth of God, then I would get on and declare it whatever awful sound the amateur organist and the seventeen octogenarian members of the congregation and myself were making, and however hilarious a speech impediment the vicar struggled with, and whatever proportion of the vocabulary in the ancient liturgy was unintelligible to me and probably those beside me on the cripplingly uncomfortable pews. It is not about comfort or polished musicians or solid exegesis or state-of-the-art technology. Although all of those things can certainly facilitate a worshipful state of mind, it is about honouring our heavenly Father.

This summer I walked into the church with the true intention of worshipping my heart out. There were some distractions, including the presence of the Archbishop of Canterbury three rows behind, sporting those distinctive eyebrows that ruin any chance he has of travelling incognito, and a man just in front who said all the liturgical responses twice as loudly as everyone else and very angrily. These issues aside, I discovered that a change in attitude made all the difference. God was honoured in that church as I am sure he is every Sunday, but on this occasion I was one of those honouring him. I found myself reflecting on it a lot afterwards.

The lady who led the prayers spoke hesitantly but from the heart. The vicar was truly ancient, but how amazing to be serving the Lord with such dedication in your latter years. His sermon was simple, but full of wisdom, and his insights into the meaning of partaking in communion have changed how I understand it and deepened my experience of it. Our singing was objectively terrible, but we did our best and the words to the hymns were glorious and rich and full of truth. It is all too easy to be a consumer and to sit there assessing the entertainment value, the sound quality, the proficiency of the leaders, the song choices and leaving with some excellent ideas for how things could be improved. In true worship, God is the consumer, not us. He is the consuming fire. He wants to consume us, to swallow us up, to burn away our sin and our self-absorption, to dazzle us into adoration and submission and gratitude.

It was good to be back in my home church at the end of the month. I am finally in a place where I fully belong to a local church. For a long time I fought the idea that I needed to be committed to a specific group of believers, but now that I am, I love it. It amazes me that so many of us show up week in week out, to meet and worship God as a group.

A Conversation with Christoph Lindner

Christoph has been on the staff team at St James' for close to a decade now, with ever growing and changing responsibilities. His musical gifting and heart for worship have been a huge blessing to our life as a church. He has directed the more traditional church choir, founded a gospel choir, set up numerous contemporary worship bands that play at our many weekly services, got the children involved in a group called 'stage crew' that performs at key times in the church year and has recorded several albums. He has an incredible singing voice, miraculously powered by lungs diseased by Cystic Fibrosis, and plays the organ, the guitar and the piano. Having flirted with the idea of finding a celebrity worship leader to interview, it struck me that I had an ideal person to talk to living round the corner, and amazingly he was able to find an available hour to get together. This is not a person with time on his hands.

I wanted to talk to Christoph specifically about sung worship, and I began by asking him why music has such spiritual significance; it seems that the idea of a connection between worship and music comes from the Bible, but what is this connection?

'You are right that this is a biblical concept – when you look at the psalms, the Jewish hymn book, they are full of instructions to sing to the Lord, to clap – all kinds of bodily expressions connected with music. God has created us not just as beings with a brain, but beings with a soul and with a heart, and singing, music in general, seems to reach the parts that other modes of expression cannot reach, to co-opt the Guinness advert! If we say something, that's alright, but if we put it to music and sing it, it will be much more connected with our emotions.'

I can be suspicious of myself when I find I am getting emotional during a song I particularly like, or when someone is doing a beautiful harmony, and I question whether it has anything to do with God, or if I am just getting into the mood as I would during a concert or driving along listening to a great tune. I asked Christoph what he would say to reassure me, or whether he thought suspicion was an appropriate stance.

Christoph seemed to feel that we can get too hung up on trying to separate out what is of God and what isn't. If we are stirred by a beautiful harmony, or a Mozart concerto or even a spectacular view, these things will speak to us of the beauty, creativity,

majesty and power of God and that's good. When he is looking at what songs to choose for a church service though, he will try to look at factors beyond how stirring they might be on a musical level, and consider how biblical the lyrics are, how they fit with where we are at spiritually as a church and so on.

I was interested to find out more about how a worship leader goes about choosing songs. Like me, you may have noticed that you can go pretty much anywhere in the world and find you are singing from the same Top Twenty Hit Worship Songs, which is oddly comforting but slightly depressing at the same time. Why do we get stuck on such a limited range of songs when the world is full of creative and musical people following God within their own incredibly diverse cultures and communities? In a provocative frame of mind, I asked Christoph if he thought that there was a clique of celebrity song writers squeezing out everyone else, and if he was bitter that he wasn't one of them. He laughed. He is not a bitter person and he was too mature to take my bait. He did have some things to say about us all getting stuck on the Hit List though:

'There are lots of positives. It expresses something of our unity in Christ. I love it when I go to another church and I don't have to sit there learning every song.

There will of course be particular centres that have immense influence. Think of Hillsong Australia – they are part of an international church movement that do big conferences where they will obviously use their songs but there is a danger of becoming monochrome. I would always want to balance those pieces, which I think we should sing in solidarity with the wider church and to help people visiting us to feel at home, with an authentic expression of worship in the local church. I love nothing more than worship songs that spring out of the local context – right where the people are and what God is saying to a

particular body of believers. I don't care if these songs are sung more widely. They might never become hits, but I think it is very important that we sing them.'

As someone who stands at the front leading the worship of a congregation, I wondered how Christoph handled the times when his heart wasn't quite in it. Was it ever ok to be mechanical about it? He thought for a moment.

'I like to think of myself as a "lead worshipper" rather than "a worship leader" – we are all worshipping together, and it is important that I am worshipping and not just performing the music because it is my job. But there are times I have led worship as an act of obedience. Now and then I don't feel like singing out songs of praise and adoration. But the good thing is that being in this ministry, being called to do it, I have to say "God I will offer you this sacrifice of praise." God will honour that. He is the same no matter what I feel.'

We chatted for a while longer, and then I wrapped up the interview by asking Christoph for a parting shot of wisdom. We both sat considering where our conversation had taken us, and his final words put everything into context for me, taking my attention back to where it belongs – to the throne of God before which we worship, and will continue to worship for all eternity:

'It helps me to see what we do from the perspective of the finish line. In Revelation it says people from every tribe, language and nation will come together before God and together raise their voices in praise of the Lamb. As the church of God, we are already, amazingly, in some time-warp way, a part of that heavenly worship. If we keep that in our sights, then all the issues about musical style and volume and song selection become fairly trite.'

The Priceless Pearl

Jesus told a story about a merchant who found a pearl of great value. In order to possess it, he sold everything he had (Matthew 13:45,46). When we worship God, we are choosing to affirm that he is worthy of our total devotion. It puts everything back in its rightful place in our minds. We are hard-wired to worship, but we don't always choose who or what we worship wisely. It is God who should have our worship. He deserves the very best of everything we have and are, and he demands loyalty and fidelity because he loves us. True love is always jealous. It always demands an undivided heart. Anyone who has ever been in love knows this – you wouldn't tolerate your beloved nurturing a crush on someone else; the very thought would make you sick to your stomach. The more we focus our attention on the Lord God, the more captivated by his beauty we will become.

I am starting to see how vital it is to worship – on my own, with my church family, with the wider church, in the beauty of creation, in the mess and trauma that life can throw up, as a decision, in the heat of an emotional moment, through my actions, with my words, with my body – every minute I am not worshipping God is a wasted minute.

CHAPTER FIVE:

SOLITUDE

*The Lord said [to Elijah], 'Go out and stand on the mountain
in the presence of the Lord, for the Lord is about to pass by.'
Then a great and powerful wind tore the mountains apart and
shattered the rocks before the Lord, but the Lord was not in the wind.
After the wind there was an earthquake, but the Lord was not in the
earthquake. After the earthquake came a fire, but the Lord was not
in the fire. And after the fire came a gentle whisper.
When Elijah heard it, he pulled his cloak over his face …*

1 KINGS 19:11–13

Henri Nouwen wrote that, 'Without solitude it is virtually impossible to live a spiritual life.'[1] I have some questions about the spiritual practice of solitude that I would like to explore with you, many of which I suspect won't have simple answers.

1. Is it really 'virtually impossible to live a spiritual life' without solitude? Where does that leave those of us for whom solitude is virtually impossible to practice?
2. Could it be valid to find solitude in peopled and noisy surroundings, simply by cultivating an inner quiet into which you can withdraw to meet with God? Might solitude be a state of mind as well as a physical reality?
3. Are some people more wired to meet God in solitude because of their personality, or is solitude something that everyone should seek

to experience?

4. Why is solitude sometimes so very uncomfortable? Why are some of us afraid of being alone?

5. Is it manipulative to make space for God and then expect him to occupy it? Surely God speaks to us at his pleasure, whether it is convenient for us or not. Or will we not hear him unless we are in a conductively deserted location?

6. Might community life be more fertile soil for spiritual growth than solitude, and perhaps even more challenging? Could the search for solitude sometimes be the spiritualisation of escapism?

There are ancient precedents for withdrawing from human society in order to meet with God. The first biblical instance I found was Isaac going out to the fields in the evening to meditate (Genesis 24:63). Moses had most of his conversations with the Almighty on the unpopulated upper slopes of Mount Sinai. Elijah spent long stretches alone in the desert, where he had frequent and dramatic encounters with the Lord. And even Jesus, who was God, withdrew to be with God, beginning his public ministry with forty days alone, and continuing to find ways of getting away from his human companions during the subsequent three years: 'Very early in the morning, while it was still dark, Jesus got up, left the house and went off to a solitary place, where he prayed' (Mark 1:35).

In most of the world's organised religions, silence is a recognised prerequisite for communicating with God. Between the third and sixth centuries, a strong emphasis on solitude emerged within the Christian tradition, as various monastic orders and individuals withdrew to the desert in order to better hear the divine whisper. There is a volume called *The Sayings of the Desert Fathers*, still in print today, which comprises accounts of several hermits' experiences collected by their contemporaries, which we can read and learn from so we don't have to do the whole desert thing ourselves.

The emphasis of Christian spirituality today seems to me to be far more outwardly focused, on community, social justice, and living a life that is transformed by our belief in Jesus. There are still people who make it a priority to have regular times away with God, but they are not in the majority. Those that do, speak of it as being essential to their spiritual health. If that is the case, what effect is the neglect of this discipline having on the rest of us? It is high time for me to make solitude in some form or another a part of my life.

Me, myself and I – not enough of a crowd

I could say with some justification that at my stage in life, solitude is unmanageable, but the truth is that I make sure to plan things fairly carefully in order to avoid being alone. When I am inescapably alone, I rarely allow the silence to be heard, or seek God in the peace. I am more likely to choose to take a nap or read a novel instead. I am not going to be too hard on myself for that while I am in my final trimester of pregnancy and running around after a 2-year-old, but I concede that there is more spiritual mileage to be covered in the spaces that occasionally do appear. I am not yet totally sold on the idea that solitude is as necessary as Henri says it is, but I am willing to have my mind changed.

You might have picked up by now that I am not one of those people whose idea of bliss is to hike up to the top of a mountain for a week by myself with only my Bible for company. My husband did this recently and came home refreshed and invigorated. I would have lasted about half an hour before joining a chatty group of amateur ramblers in the foothills.

Are you familiar with the Myers-Briggs Type Indicator? This is a system that divides people into sixteen categories based on answers given to an in-depth questionnaire about behaviour and preferences, informed by Carl Jung's theory of psychological type developed in the 1920s. It can be a useful tool for understanding yourself (and your spouse, your closest friend, your boss, your mother…) and I was interested to discover that my aversion to solitude is pretty standard for someone of my type. I am an ENFJ, which stands for Extroverted, iNtuitive, Feeling and Judging. According to one source:

'ENFJ's are so externally focused that it's especially important for them to spend time alone. This can be difficult for some ENFJs, because they have the tendency to be hard on themselves and turn to dark thoughts when alone. Consequently, ENFJs might avoid being alone, and fill their lives with activities involving other people.'[2]

On this issue I conform to type pretty closely. I have a long history of depression,[3] and when I am feeling emotionally vulnerable, being alone can tip me over the edge. In the past I have designed my life to avoid this happening, carefully scheduling plans into seamless continuity. Lately I have found a little more balance is possible without meltdown occurring, and I relish an hour or two of my own company. I don't know what would happen if this hour or two was instead a day or two, and if the only purpose of that day or two was to spend time with God. I am about to find out. I have booked a two night retreat at an Anglican convent in Wantage, and other than a daily meeting with a nun and three half-hour-long services I will be alone. Bill Hybels says that:

'God's power is available to us when we come to him in solitude, when we learn how to centre our hearts and be quiet before him. When we learn the discipline of stillness before God, we find that his leadings come through to us clearly, with little interference.'[4]

There are a couple of things that strike me about that. Firstly, he seems to be saying that this is a skill to be learned. It is not enough for me to physically isolate myself. In my aloneness I must learn to come to God, to cultivate inner quietness and in that quiet to listen and be attentive to God. Secondly, he holds out tantalising benefits to mastering this skill, namely accessing God's power, and hearing his leadings. I have to say I am fearful about these two days alone because I have never had positive experiences of solitude, but I am also excited and willing to 'feel the fear and do it anyway!'[5]

Unwanted isolation: a gift of solitude?
Some time later…

Maybe one day I will be able to experiment with solitude in the peaceful and controlled conditions of a convent. As it turns out, I wasn't able to make it this time, and instead had solitude thrust upon me as a hospital inpatient for three nights and four days. You can feel very, very alone on a busy ward I discovered, so although this was not the retreat I was expecting, it was an interesting opportunity to journey inwards and upwards.

This is how my plans were rearranged: last week I travelled to the seaside town of Eastbourne to give a seminar at a conference for Christian women. My slot was on Sunday morning and the organisers put me up in a hotel on Saturday night. I get childishly excited about staying in hotels – a key benefit of not being able to afford to stay in them very often. Unfortunately I was not able to enjoy this particular hotel experience fully because I was up all night with an unhappy stomach – I'm not sure how to put that any more delicately! The reason I mention this distasteful detail at all is because it turns out that upset tummies can provoke pre-term labour. While I gave my seminar, a kind lady in the front row timed my contractions which were fifteen minutes apart and painful enough to stop me speaking. I like to think it added some excitement to my talk – a little drama and suspense that the content alone didn't provide. By the end of Sunday I was in hospital having contractions every two minutes. I was given steroid injections to mature my baby's lungs in case she had to use them to breath six weeks earlier than scheduled, and kept in for observation. That is how I came to spend my week in hospital instead of floating around the tranquil gardens of St Mary the Virgin.

I could have made more of my hospital stay, but somehow it didn't have the same appeal as the retreat I had been anticipating. In between being hooked up to monitors, having my blood pressure taken, dealing with the discomfort of the contractions and my anxiety about the well-being of my baby, I had ample opportunity to seek God. But it didn't have the feel of a retreat; it had the feel of unwanted confinement and isolation. I was lonely. And it was one of those times that any sense of the reality of God's presence with me failed to register on an emotional level. What I heard in the silence was more silence. Actually, it wasn't technically very silent what with the screams of women in labour and the moans of the poor men who had to watch (HA!).

I would start filling the space with words, gabbling away to God about this and that. After a while I would read an edifying book and a while after that I would go and get a cup of tea and get distracted reading the magazines in the tea room and chatting with the other patients who weren't imminently giving birth. This was a cycle that I went through many times a day and less energetically during the night. I felt very frustrated with myself for not making more of this chance to be alone and not having very much of substance to report to you.

I like the thought of being able to turn a lonely season into an opportunity for spiritual adventure. I know that there are people who have the maturity and discipline to do just this, and the world benefits from their prayers in ways we can only guess at. But I have nothing but sympathy for those who can only feel the pain. Loneliness is a terrible thing. It is all very well to take yourself away from human society for a self-determined period of time for the purpose of seeking God, but it feels very different when you haven't chosen it and can't end it.

Finding solitude where it may be found

What a lot can happen between two paragraphs! I have come back to this writing project after giving birth to a second little daughter, Charis Eden, who arrived at full term weighing 7lb 1oz, and is now four months old: smiley, delightful and not very quiet. My life has less silence and less time than it did, and I find I treasure the limited solitude that comes my way. According to economic theory, scarcity drives up value, and economic theory definitely applies here! The girl who would once go to great lengths to avoid her own company now craves it. Three times a week, I leave the house for twenty minutes on my own to run or rather wobble, around the neighbourhood. These are my times for uninterrupted communion with God. I ignore the pain in my calves and lungs as best I can. I am not plugged into any music-making device. I relish the fact that I am not lugging bags of baby equipment, that the only nose I have to wipe is my own and that if God wants to speak to me he has my attention. The other day I thought he might have told me that it is OK for me to just rest in his company. I really needed to hear that, and ever since I have felt released from the pressure to make long-winded speeches to him all the time. I manage to get out for these runs because my husband is willing to have both girls while he has his breakfast three days a week. It can be a bit of a stretch for both of us to achieve, but somehow it happens.

You may think that finding time alone would be impossible in your circumstances, but could you take another look and perhaps get a bit creative? Maybe there are windows of time that you just haven't identified, or realised the potential of. Most of us find time to shower, and do it on our own (personally I always have an audience of two little girls, but I cherish the thought of one day regaining my bathroom privacy). Where is your mind as you scrub the dirt from your body? Could this be your sacred space? How about your commute to work? Are you one of the dying breed who still iron their clothes? Could you meet God over the ironing board? Could you stand to forgo the TV one evening a week and let silence surround you until bedtime? What about those times you are driving somewhere and the baby falls asleep in the back and space opens up like the road ahead?

Carving out time for solitude

My original plan for several days and nights away in a convent is not feasible at the moment, and so I am scaling down my expectations and I am going on a one day retreat instead. It has been a bit of a logistical headache to delegate my responsibilities on the home front, but I have managed it. I've been inspired to do so by the fact that my mother and my friend Ally, both mothers of four, were able to make it work even when their broods were young. If something is important enough then there are often ways and means of doing it.

When you start looking, you will find there are bountiful options for places to go to spend unhurried, uninterrupted time with God. If you are blessed to live in an amenable climate, you can always just head out into the great outdoors. Many religious communities will be open to sojourners for varying lengths of time. You could go and use a friend's house while they are out (best to get permission first, or be sure to clean up very thoroughly when you leave and take treats for the dog). When I was planning my day I knew I wanted to leave my house and actually go somewhere. I could have stayed at home, but the laundry and the dust would have been clamouring for my attention, and anyway, it would have seemed a bit anticlimactic, like getting a Chinese take-away in to celebrate your ten year wedding anniversary. I found a retreat house an hour's drive away that looked promising, and booked a room for the day.

My expectations of these hours away were low. I thought it would be hard, that I would feel fidgety and uncomfortable, and frustrated with myself for not making the most of an opportunity to listen to God. I took my laptop, and planned to use the last couple of hours to work. I worked out an agenda – the key items that I wished the Lord to address in my life and I stumbled on the morning like someone arriving late at a job interview, scruffy, under-prepared and yet still hoping for favourable reception.

The first thing that happened was that five minutes into the journey I began to feel peaceful and relaxed. I noticed that the sky was perfectly blue for the first time this year and the air was warm and full of pollen, which is a good thing when you don't have hay fever – it just makes everything smell summery and nice. I sensed that God was not going to keep to my agenda. I think he said to me, 'Let's just spend time together – I like you and that sounds fun!' I began to think about the friendship that Jesus had with Mary, Martha and Lazarus, and the house at Bethany where he seemed so at home. I have always identified with Martha in the story of his dinner there, the cross and controlling older sister, but maybe I could learn to sit and be with Jesus as Mary did. Jesus said that this was the one thing that is needed (Luke 10:41). How simple he made it sound. Maybe it is that simple.

Stanton House is a gracefully proportioned red brick stately home in lush green grounds. There is a stream, a fruit garden, a meadow with horses standing around eating flowers and views of gentle English hills. I was given the prayer room as a base, but as the weather was so beautiful I spent most of my time outside. In case you think this all sounds too good to be true, let me insert into the picture the grass-cutting tractor that seemed to follow me everywhere I went, belching out petrol fumes and noise, and the little old ladies on folding chairs dotted around the place on a group retreat with their church!

The morning passed by in a dreamlike way, as I discovered that it is possible to enjoy spending time with God. You don't have to try, you don't have to fill up the time with words or worry about concentrating. You can just be in his presence. I was almost dizzy with amazement that this is the case and that I have taken so long to find it out. I was still mulling over the relationship that Mary had with Jesus, and how extravagantly she loved him. I didn't have a pint of perfume to pour over him, but it occurred to me that my most precious commodity right now is time, and I decided that I would give him the whole day and do no work at all. The book deadline is very close now and so this was more of a sacrifice than it maybe sounds.

Then, because the opportunity was too good to miss, I took a nap on the floor of my prayer room. After I woke up and didn't have lunch (I was fasting, mainly because the dining room was full with the ladies) I followed an outline for three hours of prayer written by Tricia McCary Rhodes.[6] This led me through a time of reflection, petition and finally looking ahead.

Before I headed home I tried to capture what today had been about in my journal. The last thing I wrote was, 'I heard the Lord say to me today, "It is good for us to be together. I am enough. Only one thing is needed."'

When Peter saw Jesus transfigured up the mountain, his instinct was to set up camp and stay there (Mark 9:5). I would have jumped at the chance to stay a bit longer at Stanton House, but my time was up. I headed home scheming about how I could make space in my life for regular retreats. I have shocked myself by finding a day alone with God to be a wonderful thing.

I wanted to give you a flavour of what a longer retreat might be like, so I asked around and found someone to talk to. Tim is someone who is comfortable in his own company but he had never gone away alone to be with God before.

He chose a retreat centre near Liverpool and joined a group of ten others on a week-long silent retreat. Each day he would have a twenty minute meeting with a spiritual director, who gave him four verses to meditate on. The next day he would tell her how God had spoken through those verses and she'd prayerfully give him four more. Other than this brief interaction the time was spent alone – or rather, in the company of the Lord. All he had with him was a Bible, and as the time went by he slowed down, able to put aside the outside world and his inner distractions. He felt there was a great benefit to having taken a longer time out of his schedule, since he needed the stretch of days rather than hours to 'detox' and get into the rhythm of stillness. I asked him if it was daunting waking up each morning and facing so much empty space, but his reply was: 'Existing in active and direct communication with God made for a full day – it didn't feel empty… Silence is not empty. Silence is full of God.'

Inner Quiet: Alone in a Crowd

I have come to the rather obvious conclusion that to experience solitude you need to be alone. But I do think that we could make more of the private world of our own minds, a room that is available to us to withdraw into at any time. Even if just for a few seconds, we can pull back from what is going on around us and touch base with God in the sanctuary of our consciousness. I include this concept of solitude because in some seasons that may be all we can manage, and because I think that baby steps are OK – for some of us an hour, let alone a week or a month, of time alone with God is too much, so we need to begin with seconds and work up. From my conversations with people who 'do' solitude frequently, there are significant benefits from longer stints. I understand that, but we all have to start somewhere.

Sometimes the fruit of longer times of solitude is the ability to capture the moments more easily. I once had the pleasure of an American speaker's company over breakfast at a conference. Her first encounter with solitude had been during a long-term illness when she had sensed God telling her she was not to have any visitors. She spent six weeks in total seclusion, wounding and offending scores of family and friends who badly wanted to be with her and care for her. By the time she emerged, she had discovered a depth of relationship with God that made her long to retreat from the world again. She told me that she now finds she can create quiet inward places to commune with the Lord pretty much anywhere.

Libby Black: One of God's Favourites

There are some people who find solitude so compelling that they find they crave more and more of it. *A Book of Silence*[7] by Sara Maitland chronicles her progression from living a noisy, sociable existence to her new life alone on the Isle of Skye. It is a fascinating account of her growing love and understanding of what it means to withdraw from human society, covering the cultural and religious background of silence, and considering with great frankness both the benefits and the dangers of self-imposed isolation. She is taking herself to the outer extremities of aloneness with God, and it makes frightening and intriguing reading. I thought that she would be a good person to interview, but perhaps predictably my communications were met with.... silence! Perhaps it was all for the best, because instead of finding someone who practices solitude like an extreme sport, I have found someone to talk to whom we will more easily relate – my friend Libby.

I know Libby from church – she is someone with a vast and varied experience of solitude. For many years she has lived and worked in Bulstrode, a stately home that houses the headquarters of WEC, which stands for World Evangelisation for Christ. She is someone who very much enjoys her own company so living and eating with sixty people day in day out has been a challenge for her. Recently she moved into a brand new one-bedroom flat in the grounds, and the evening we met for our chat was my first opportunity to see it for myself. She showed me around with sparkling eyes, pointing out the particularly exciting features with a tone of disbelief: an ensuite bathroom, a little study that she can use to do her crafts, a light and airy kitchen and living area, and most significant of all, a front door that she can close at the end of the day.

'I love to be alone and have quietness and space after a busy day. It can be very hectic in the main building, even in the evenings. Living in this new home, I sense God's presence in the stillness and calm, and I can really relax.'

Each day for Libby begins with prayer and Bible reading. If time is short, she will prioritise this over breakfast. Amazing! Libby defines solitude as time alone spent with God, and for her it is a central and vital part of being a Christian. She feels that if we don't make space to be alone with God, we risk missing what he has to say to us.

Being alone was not always a spiritual experience for Libby, or even a positive one. She grew up with four brothers and three sisters, in a family that was often emotionally bruising and difficult. She would retreat to her bedroom and sleep for hours at a time to escape her feelings of hurt. Solitude was a form of self-protection, her way of coping with her fraught surroundings. Occasionally she still fights the impulse to withdraw in this way, but mostly she seeks space with a different motivation these days. At nineteen years old she became a Christian, and began to find God in the silence. She still longed to be alone, but now it was because it was when she was alone that she most felt God's presence and heard him speaking to her. It became a source of deep satisfaction and joy.

I vividly remember a short conversation we had in the run up to a holiday Libby took a couple of years ago. She was fizzing with excitement at the prospect of two weeks entirely alone, house-sitting for friends who were away, and I was baffled. I asked her again about that unusual choice of vacation:

'I surprised myself. I would never have imagined I would have done something like that, staying in someone else's home while they were away, and being entirely on my own for two weeks. But it was...WOW... a rich experience! I sat out in the garden, and went for walks, I prayed and read the Bible, and just sat listening to God. I knew no one would knock on the door and disturb me, so I could sink into the silence and enjoy it.'

This was a season of solitude that Libby had chosen, prepared for and entered into with great anticipation. Recently though, she had a long period of solitude thrust upon her by ill health. She was unable to walk or even stand without fainting or vomiting, and for several long weeks her world shrunk to the size of her bedroom. She had visitors, but the majority of the time was spent by herself. These circumstances were far from ideal, and I wanted to know whether it had been harder for her to look for the spiritual potential in this sort of aloneness than the kind you deliberately seek out. For Libby, looking to God was her only option, and it seems that having got her full attention by confining her to her bedroom, he used the time to do some important work in her:

'I wanted to be open to God and allow him to speak, and that is exactly what he did. I look back and think that I wouldn't have the freedom I do now if my illness hadn't happened. When you have something precious, like an antique, you need to care for it and maintain it. I felt like God was restoring me like a precious possession. I sensed his presence so strongly it was like he was standing in my room. Someone who had come to visit prayed that God would mend my broken heart, that he would give me a warm, whole heart. I could almost feel it happening. I honestly believe that God has given me a new heart.'

I asked her if there is always potential for a time of unwanted isolation to bear fruit. What advice would she give to people who are struggling to turn things around?

'Yes – I believe that God uses everything for good. Try and be still. Listen to quiet music, immerse yourself in Scripture, take upon you every promise he has given you. Listen for his voice – I am sure he will say something. Look for what God is doing in that time; he is always at work. He takes every opportunity that comes along. He doesn't waste any time. I just know that he will do something beautiful in you.'

Reflections

It has been interesting for me to listen to someone who finds solitude so blissful, invigorating and rich, because it still scares me. I know that Libby probably has a temperament that predisposes her finding silence restful, and also that her life circumstances, particularly the fact that she is unmarried (thus far – who knows what might happen…) have given her scope to develop this discipline. But it has confirmed to me more strongly than ever that this is something I can't avoid if I want to have an intimate relationship with God.

CHAPTER SIX

SIMPLICITY

He has shown all you people what is good.
And what does the Lord require of you?
To act justly and to love mercy
and to walk humbly with your God.

MICAH 6:8

Living for God is not complicated. The prophet Micah captured the essence of what it involves – to act justly, love mercy, and walk humbly with God. And yet, as Jesus talked about in his parable of the sower, our lives do need to be cultivated to make them a context in which faith can flourish – soil in which the seed of God's Word will grow strong and bear fruit. This is where simplicity as a Christian discipline comes in. Certain complications of life are weeds that will choke our spiritual life if we don't do some serious gardening.

Simplicity might sound like a romantic and desirable state, particularly if you are standing on a crowded underground platform trying to contain your rising panic about how much you need to achieve in the following nine hours. I have always thought that advertisements for holidays in remote Scottish Castles stuck to the walls of these grimy tunnels must be devastatingly effective. Every now and then it becomes fashionable to live simply, although when it is a lifestyle choice not a necessity it can be a costly business. Of course, if you can afford to outsource your ironing, employ a nutritionist to decide and deliver your simple weekly menus, and delegate your wardrobe management to a stylist then life is going to be easier and space will be freed up to 'just be'. For most of us, attaining a simple life is going to take more than increasing our paid staff. It is going to entail prioritising and sacrifice, thought, focus and perseverance. Simplicity is not a naturally occurring phenomenon – left alone, life will get more complicated not less. You can test that theory by sitting in an armchair for a few hours and watching things spiral out of control. But it is one in which there is greater freedom to put one foot in front of the other and get on with the business of walking humbly with God.

In Isaiah 30:15, the Lord, speaking to Israel through the prophet Isaiah, said this: 'In repentance and rest is your salvation, in quietness and trust is your strength.'

They were under huge stress and in a painfully ironic act of disobedience, had formed an alliance with Egypt rather than seeking their security from God. Repentance, rest, quietness, trust – this is what makes up a life lived simply in obedience to God.

I am going to try and simplify four areas of my life this month – my physical surroundings, my use of time, my inner monologue and my relationships. There will be some visible changes, but I see the most important challenge to be about my attitude and my approach towards what is there, rather than attempting to get rid of things.

Week One

Material simplicity: the challenge of letting go
You may not be aware of this, but my full name and title is 'Jo Swinney, Queen of Clutter and Ruler of the Never-ending Sea of Homeless Stuff.' Everywhere I have ever lived has been silted up around the edges with odd socks, old bank statements, tangled up necklaces and

other carefully hoarded detritus. When I was at boarding school I travelled back to Portugal each holiday with giant suitcases full of quite randomly selected possessions. On one occasion, my grandparents came to pick me up to take me to the airport and I met them in the hallway of my boarding house with a giant brown case that I could barely lift. They went on strike and refused to put it in the car. Fireworks ensued, but eventually I was persuaded to downsize and leave behind a couple of text books and some dirty school uniform. It could be a family trait – my brother used to bring home his hockey stick for the holidays.

When I moved to Canada after university, I stored several boxes of stuff in my aunt and uncle's cellar. Four years later when I returned to collect my long-lost possessions I found myself questioning the sanity of the person (me) who had decided this shabby, mismatched and now mouldy collection was worth keeping. Why did I think it so important to hang onto the lava lamp, the stained red and green horse cushion cover, the teddy bear tin full of paper clips and decaying plastic bands, the tea-stained mugs and chipped plates that had seen me through my student years when functionality overruled aesthetics? What I was doing was imbuing these objects with the significance of the stories that had brought them into my life. The tin, which I have to confess I have hung onto and can see from where I now sit, lived in my room at home in Portugal, came with me and spent five years in different locations at school, took a short sabbatical in storage while I went off to Africa and was back in action again once I started at university. It is not a pretty tin. I can't even remember how I came to have it, and I can go for years never needing anything that is stored within it, but I am not about to get rid of it. You could replicate this scenario with dozens of other items, and that is part of why I am surrounded by piles that grow and shrink but never go away.

Another part of it is because I grew up worrying about money. My parents founded a charity and were paid a very modest salary by a mission organisation, on which we managed just fine. But I was aware that if I set my heart on wanting anything expensive, I would most likely be frustrated, so I decided to try not to want things. And I hung onto the things I already had long after they had intrinsic worth. All of this means that when Shawn and I decided a few weeks ago to have a declutter ahead of moving house, it was a monumental task, both on a practical level and, for me, on an emotional and spiritual level too.

Stuff saps energy. It needs organising, tidying, and maintaining. It takes thought, space, money and attention. When we die, other people have to disperse it and they may think ill of the dead as they make their ninth trip to the charity shop. My grandmother – she of the suitcase incident – turned out to have accumulated a staggeringly large collection of shoes and matching handbags over her adult life. She loved to shop, had a great eye for a bargain, and she always looked fantastic, but I am sure even she must have wondered if things had gone a bit far. Why do we persist in acquiring more than we need, and in keeping things that have no use and may even get in our way, literally or figuratively? I have explained some of my reasons. How about yours? We are all targeted by advertising that is aimed to generate dissatisfaction that can be eased by a new product. We are all susceptible to the sin of covetousness; maybe we can take or leave our neighbours' donkey, but their convertible is another story. We all think that buying things will scratch our itch for adventure and cure the boredom, albeit temporarily. We all occasionally believe the lie that there is a connection between our worth and the monetary value of what we have.

We can end up being full-time curator in a personal museum of useless stuff; do we really want that job? Or does it sound like a better idea to be free to come and go, to enjoy the exhibits and to let other people enjoy them too?

Back to the GREAT DECLUTTER OF 2010... This week has only touched the surface and shown me how big a job has to be done. But I have got into the swing of things. So far, three car loads have gone to the big local recycling depot, a car load has gone to one of the 500 charity shops (give or take) on the high street, and the front hall is piled high with boxes of things that I want to find new homes for. I have become increasingly reckless and abandoned. Alexa has been hovering anxiously over each box and bin bag, peering in and occasionally rescuing an object that is inexplicably precious to her (attachments to junk begin early). I tried and failed on three separate occasions to get rid of a small one-eared metal bunny rabbit with a Sunday school sticker wrapped around it and a bell in its tummy. She could hear that bell alerting her to its danger from any room in the house. In the end I allowed her to keep the bunny. It is OK to be fond of our possessions. It is right that we appreciate beauty and quality: all good things come from above. But it is also good and right to assert our allegiance to the creator by letting stuff go every now and then, even if it is uncomfortable to do so.

If you are considering the spiritual discipline of decluttering, here are some tips that I have picked up:

1. Give yourself a time limit for the big jobs, and tackle them one at a time.
2. Ask yourself if there is someone who needs what you have more than you do.
3. Fill up a box with things that have no home but which you are not ready to get rid of. Put it away for three months. If you can remember what is in it and have missed it, you can keep it. Otherwise, get rid of it.
4. You have three categories: Keep and Use. Recycle (or throw away if you have to, bearing in mind that there is no such place as 'away')[1]. Give Away. Put everything in your home into one of these categories.

Jesus said:

'Do not store up for yourselves treasures on earth, where moth and rust destroy, and where thieves break in and steal. But store up for yourselves treasures in heaven...For where your treasure is, there your heart will be also.' (Matthew 6:19–21)

Treasures on earth are beguiling and addictive, but they don't last. The pain of letting go is worth it.

Week Two

Simple schedule: the challenge of time management

I like to be busy. My busyness is a strategy for coping with long hours of childcare, it is a way of preventing myself from becoming too introspective and to some degree it is how I justify my existence. My diary is generally a rather hectic and battered-looking object, and if I ever lost it I would be in serious mental discomfort. As it turned out, I didn't have to take a decision to draw a line through the activities of a week; the decision was made for me when both little girls got ill and we were quarantined. For nine days we went nowhere and saw no one. Aaah – the simple life!

While a lot of the time dragged by excruciatingly slowly, I gradually adjusted to my new, unstructured way of being and began to enjoy some unexpected benefits. Once she had stopped vomiting and regained her appetite, Alexa's boredom flowered into imaginative play that had her taking beach holidays in the hallway, caring tenderly for sick teddies and carrying out long and chatty phone calls on her pink plastic mobile. I stopped looking at the clock, and did some of the jobs that sit at the bottom of every list I make and never get ticked off; I even washed the kitchen walls. I felt quieter and calmer.

Every now and then, it can be a good idea to step off the treadmill entirely and get some perspective on the speed at which we have been travelling. Almost every summer of my life I have spent at least a couple of weeks in Pembrokeshire, on the beautiful coast of West Wales. The elements of a day reduce to eating, swimming, walking, reading and napping. It is a beautiful existence. But there comes a day when I realise I am ready to return to the fray. Uncluttered time is a luxury and I suspect that those who live in it for more than a season will eventually find it unsatisfying. When I was travelling around East Africa as a 19-year-old, I met all sorts of people in backpackers' hostels drifting around the world like flotsam in a lifelong pursuit of hedonistic simplicity – no regular bills, no relational obligations, no political involvement, no time commitments, no valuable possessions. Even then, I knew not to envy them. I thought that they were trying to stay asleep to make a dream last, and that never works. I think that work and activity and movement are good things. Work was there in the unblemished pre-fall creation. It took up six days of every seven. I don't imagine for a second that Adam and Eve petitioned God for more time to sit around doing nothing. I expect they rather liked their lives. So I am not advocating a sprituality of laziness. What I do think though is that we don't necessarily put enough thought or discernment into the elements that make up our days, and often take on commitments that we are driven to do rather than *called* to do.[2]

During my nine home-bound days I pondered how and why a simplified schedule might be considered spiritually beneficial. I concluded that it was perhaps more to do with the peace that results from only doing the things that we should be doing. Discerning what those things are is not always straightforward. Is it self-indulgent to include lots of unproductive white-space on our calenders? Can we justify saying no to requests for help when technically we are not doing anything else on that particular day? Each decision needs to be made individually, but the guiding principle is to discover what God might like us to do, not just what we feel we have to do to please people or justify our oxygen intake. The will of God is not a mystery. Paul writes this to the Romans:

Do not conform to the pattern of this world, but be transformed by the renewing of your mind. Then you will be able to test and approve what God's will is – his good, pleasing and perfect will. (Romans 12:2)

Our transformation is a life-long process, but as we become more like Jesus, we will begin to think like him, and know instinctively when to say 'yes' and when to say 'no'. Most people I know have more trouble saying no, so perhaps it is worth emphasising: 'no' is sometimes what God's will requires us to say.

If we find we are feeling stressed, scattered, guilty and stretched much of the time, our commitments need to be reassessed. I ended up taking some actions as a result of those empty days. I left a committee, I rejoined a Bible study group and I decided to pull out of a monthly group that I can't identify because I actually haven't had the guts to make the call yet and maybe by the time the book hits the shelves I will still be resentfully attending.

Week Three

Simple attitude: the challenge of contentment
Simplicity perhaps has more to do with internals than externals. Paul wrote this: 'I have learned the secret of being content in any and every situation, whether well fed or hungry, whether living in plenty or in want. I can do all this through him who gives me strength' (Philippians 4:12,13). Could it be that we can live simply just by cultivating a grateful mindset? What we think always translates to how we behave, but we do not always have total control over our environment. What we can gain control over is our minds.

This week I was given a wonderful opportunity to discipline my mind and bend it into submission. The house I live in is provided by the church Shawn works for, as a part of his salary package. It is a three-storey terrace, with no garden, and in some ways it has been a challenging home to raise a family in – of course I am speaking relatively here. I do realise how ridiculous what I have just said will sound to the majority of the world whose housing is not adequate, let alone ideal (if they even have housing, which many don't). But the challenge is to grow godly characters in the soil we are planted in, and my soil is South Buckinghamshire, where not having a garden is a deprivation. I might have managed to be more accepting of the quirks of Number 7, but when I was pregnant with Alexa, over three years ago, our very loving and thoughtful church began to say the accommodation wasn't suitable for a family and plans to move us were afoot. It has been an agonisingly slow process, but last month we were shown around the most beautiful new home we could have ever asked for and told that we could be moving as soon as three weeks hence. Then the sale of our house fell through, and the other house went back on the market about five minutes later.

While the prospect of a move was a vague idea, I worked hard on being content, not wanting to fall into the trap of the old woman who lived in a shoe but still wasn't happy when she was magically relocated to a palace. I figured if I didn't learn to appreciate this house, I would probably find fault with anywhere I lived. Since a move looked a more definite proposition though, I allowed myself to gripe about the poorly laid out space, the mouldy bathroom and the blistered kitchen counters (sadly, those were the fault of my stove-top coffee maker. The stove-top coffee maker being an inanimate object, I suppose it cannot take all the blame. That would rightly belong to the person who put it down on the non-heat-resistant work top: me). The day we heard that things were not going ahead as planned was a bad day. It really threw me. I did not want to be content in this house any more. I wanted to move into a beautiful new house and be content there. I spent several days in a state of agitation and sadness. Romans 8 verses 28 and 29 is a promise that God has kept in my life any time I have shown willingness to let him work on me through difficult things: 'And we know that in all things God works for the good of those who love him, who have been called according to his purpose. For those God foreknew he also predestined to be conformed to the image of his Son...' Somehow, a house had shuffled its way onto centre-stage and stolen the limelight that ought to have been occupied by Jesus. The swift exit stage right had left me feeling empty and deflated, and I knew I was reacting disproportionately for someone who professed to be rooted and established in Christ. It was an opportunity to refocus, and I have taken it.

I feel a little sheepish bringing you into the details of this pedestrian saga, because although I feel it has been a spiritually significant process for me, it is not particularly dramatic. I decided to share it anyway though, because I found it exciting that even the minor hiccups in life offer the chance for God to transform us into his Son's likeness. I think that we really can learn to be content in any situation, if our joy is coming from intimacy with our creator. If we can internalise this truth, our fears lose their hold.

What is going on in your life that is getting you gnarled up right now? Are you waiting for something, perhaps the results of a medical test, perhaps the outcome of an interview, or maybe the next visit from a far-flung family member? So much of life seems to be about waiting and often the waiting feels like wasted time; we sit on hold, listening to that maddening jingle, accomplishing nothing. I would like to challenge you to take this situation and ask God to help you find contentment now, in this moment. I believe this is the key to a life of inner simplicity.

Week Four

Simple relationships: the challenge of authenticity

Relationships are not straightforward. Think for a moment about just a few of the factors that come into play as we interact with other

members of our species:
- We want to be liked and approved of.
- We often have unarticulated motivations for maintaining a friendship, such as enjoying feeling needed, or looking like the thin person by comparison, or hoping to benefit from a person's connections.
- Everybody is damaged to some extent, and will in turn do damage. It is not particularly safe to get involved with anybody.
- We assume common ground, but we are all standing on our own bit of ground, seeing things from a unique perspective.
- Some people have more power than others.

Every day is spent relating to other people in one way or another. We will probably deal with work colleagues, people taking our money in exchange for things we need or want, family members, friends, vague acquaintances and so on. Social networking sites such as Facebook mean we will be in touch with some pretty random updates from a wide range of sources. I have 386 'friends'. Obviously this is stretching the definition of friendship beyond its traditionally understood meaning.

I spent this week trying to be particularly aware of my relationships, and where and why they felt complicated. First thing on Monday morning, I handed in a letter to the head of Alexa's nursery explaining that she would be going to a different nursery next term. I felt awful about this – it was something I dreaded doing, even though the reasons for it were very clear and not at all personal. The fact is I felt I had got to know the head teacher; I liked her, and I felt I was letting her down. On Tuesday, I took Charis (now six months old) over to my friend who has agreed to look after her one morning a week until the book deadline. I am not doing anything for her in return, and this makes me feel very uneasy. Later that day a couple I have only met once came for lunch to discuss a vision they have for helping churches support depressed people. I intended to make soup and bread, and ended up buying soup and bread, which I know is not the end of the world, but I felt I had offered substandard hospitality. My sister and her husband had been staying all week because a volcano in Iceland prevented them from leaving on their round the world trip. On Wednesday, she mentioned that they might like to live in New Zealand for a few years. I irrationally took this as a personal rejection, and told her in so many words that if she did that it would be extremely selfish. Thursday's challenge was the discovery that my neighbour was breaking the law in a way I can't reveal here in case I incriminate myself, and trying to figure out what I should do about it. I ended up speaking to her, as lovingly as I could, about why I was worried about what she was doing, knowing that I was risking undermining a carefully nurtured friendship. On Friday I bumped into the postman three times and by the third time it was definitely a little awkward. On Saturday I lost my temper with Alexa and felt like a terrible mother (of a terrible child). On Sunday I had dozens of unsatisfactory half conversations after church and spent a considerable amount of time afterwards thinking of things I should have said or not said.

During the week there were numerous times I encountered needs that I did not meet, felt hurt, said thoughtless or insensitive things, put on a persona with people I don't feel comfortable being myself with, invested emotional energy on small and insignificant encounters and neglected key friendships. The way we relate to others has everything to do with the way we relate to God, and how we handle our relationships matters hugely to him. Six of the Ten Commandments refer to our relationships with people. Jesus said that the crux of the Law and the Prophets was loving God and loving each other (Matthew 22:37–40). Part of the quest for holiness must therefore involve a careful look at how we are conducting our human relationships. Are we loving, honest, forgiving, generous, sensitive, and generally as Christ-like as we can be towards the people in our lives? Am I? Regretfully, no. But I am going to continue working on it.

How might we be able to simplify our relationships? I have a few ideas.

- We need to care more about what God thinks of us than what people think. This is going to take a very long time to achieve, but needs to be our goal so that we can have genuine freedom in the way we relate to others.

- We would probably all benefit from an audit of the people in our lives. Who are we close to? Are these relationships positive and helpful? Are we spreading ourselves too thinly? Are there any relationships that could use a bit of investment? Are there any people we should consider distancing ourselves from?
- We can do our best to give without resentment and receive without guilt.
- We can treat everybody in our lives in a way that reflects the fact that they are God's beloved creation.
- We can discipline ourselves to forgive every wrong that is done to us and to be quick to recognise when we are in the wrong.

As a person who is sensitive, analytical and pretty sociable, this is a very tricky area for me. This week has made me realise just how much work I need to do to make my relationships glorifying to God.

A Conversation with Fiona Castle

I sought out Fiona Castle a few years ago as I began to take on more speaking and writing assignments. She lives nearby, and I wanted a mentor who would help me navigate the pitfalls, in particular the dual dangers of insecurity and arrogance. Fiona is wonderfully grounded and humble and has become a lovely friend as well as a source of wisdom and encouragement. She agreed to discuss simplicity with me, the subject of one of her books,[3] and we sat down together one evening last week after I had got the girls into bed. Simplicity has been very important to Fiona ever since she took a trip to Latin America in her sixties. She had previously visited Calcutta with the Oasis Trust, a charity of which she was a patron, but other than that her life had been pretty sheltered from extreme poverty. I asked her about the impact of this visit:

'My daughter Julia had been living in Peru for some time, and I was quite reluctant to go and visit her because she was living in a shanty town in very simple surroundings in the poorest area of the outskirts of Lima and I knew what I was in for if I went, so I kept making excuses. Eventually I realised she was feeling quite rejected so I plucked up the courage and went, and it was a life-changing experience. What I discovered was not the poverty, which is very obvious, but the generosity of spirit which we seem to have lost in the west. We are so bound up by things and material gain, and we are not thinking about people. When you don't have things, you care about people and I noticed that they really cared about one another and supported each other and were involved in each other's lives. I was totally challenged when I came home to declutter my life, to make it much more straightforward.'

I wondered what practical things had changed as a result of this resolution. Did she consider radically downsizing – perhaps moving into her garden shed?

'I have to live within my own culture. I couldn't live in a shed at the bottom of the garden because I wouldn't have been taken seriously. What I wanted to focus on was what is really important and not what to buy next. There are so many makeover programmes about homes and gardens and clothes and they make us feel inadequate. They make us hanker after what we don't have, thinking these things will make us feel better. I just wanted to dump all of that.'

I understood the direction she was taking, but I also felt that maybe the issue was more complex. The material world is good and God is glorified through beauty and quality, and dare I say it, cares about how things look and feel and smell. Think of the detail with which he described how he wanted his temple – the metals, the stones, the colours, the shapes were all important to him. If the goal of your life is acquiring possessions, that is idolatrous, but throwing it all off is surely not quite right either. Fiona wasn't willing to allow me any sanctified materialism though:

'I think you can appreciate beauty in nature.'

I pushed her a little. How about a well-made sofa or a beautifully knitted sweater?

'I can always appreciate those things! But to have to have it because it is the latest fashion is not necessary. I have enough clothes in my wardrobe to see me out now. So why am I worried about my clothes? I want to be able to use my money in a more generous way and a wiser way. God called us to lay everything down in order to follow him. That doesn't mean living a pauper's life, but focusing on what is really important to him is what has really challenged me as a result of my experience in Peru.

There is such a difference between what we need and what we want. When I was with Julia in Peru, her home only had orange boxes on their sides lined with newspaper as furniture. Being a generous mum and wanting to indulge my daughter who I didn't see very often I wanted to buy her a new set of shelves and a wardrobe and a kitchen cupboard. She said, "Mum, you just don't get it. I have everything I need." That was such a rap on the knuckles for me because she did have what she needed. She coped. She survived. She got on with her life. But she was so free. There were so many times that people would show up at three in the morning and she'd be available and there for them. She was able to be what God wanted her to be in those circumstances.

I feel that we all in this nation need to live more simply, live within our means, only pay for what we can afford and go without. I was born and brought up during the second world war and clothes and food were on ration. When I was a teenager I used to save up for months and months for things I saw in the

shops, and hope they would still be there when I could afford them. It meant that I appreciated everything so much more.'

Fiona was married to the late Roy Castle, who worked in show business and was a household name in Britain for many years. I was curious about whether she had been drawn into the appearance-obsessed celebrity culture that often comes with the territory of fame and success.

'I was never drawn into show business. Roy recognised that he was very lucky to earn a living doing something he loved. For him it was about earning a living, not about being famous or being seen in the right places – it never interested us. We lived a very ordinary, boring life. We didn't do anything to seek publicity. I was also in show business in a much lower strata. There was a lovely saying in the theatre in those days – "You had better be nice to people on the way up because you are bound to meet them on the way down"'

Simple Simon: Role Model for the Wise?

In the nursery rhyme, Simple Simon asks the pie man for a pie, not realising that he needs money to pay for it. Godly simplicity does not entail a denial of the complex realities of life. We need to engage with our circumstances, our environment, our relationships and our responsibilities. But there is perhaps a way we can do it that allows us to have a stillness at our centre, a place deep inside that is tranquil and attuned to the voice of God saying, 'This is the way; walk in it' (Isaiah 30:21).

END NOTES

*His divine power has given us everything
we need for a godly life.*

2 PETER 1:3

This journey has taken me longer than the six months I had planned, because of the issues during my late pregnancy and then the sheer exhaustion that followed the birth. But what I am really glad to be able to say is that I have travelled a little way along the road, even with all the detours and time spent in lay-bys. It has not been just a gimmick. Doing spiritual disciplines has brought me closer to God. I think we know each other better now than we did last year. And I am excited about what comes next: 'Forgetting what is behind and straining towards what is ahead, I press on towards the goal to win the prize for which God has called me heavenwards in Christ Jesus' (Philippians 3:13,14).

What's Stuck?

I'd love to say that I have kept going with every discipline I've played with during these past few months. I can't say that, because it wouldn't be true. Some have stuck, but a good many have fallen by the wayside. I could take a negative tack here, berate myself, don a camel skin garment and go weeping into the desert yowling about my failure, or I could celebrate the good that has come from this experiment.

Let me begin with a look at what I do now that I did not do before. I have adopted the practice of fasting from the Internet every Sunday, as a symbolic gesture to God that I want to give him my full attention and because I want to challenge my addictive tendencies. I have tentatively tried a couple of short food fasts because I think I am beginning to understand why denying oneself food has a spiritual impact. And I have had another week-long fiction fast, during which time I read some amazingly edifying Christian literature.

My frazzled brain cells have managed to retain some of the Scripture that I memorised, and God has used it to speak to me on numerous occasions, which has spurred me on to commit more to memory. I have found that my imagination has become more engaged with my reading of the Bible, particularly the Gospels. I am reading more slowly, and trying to capture the atmosphere, the sounds, the smells and the emotions that flicker like candle-shadows behind the words.

I have started to go running again, now that my body is somewhat recovered from the birth, and I pray as I run. I have found my prayer life has become more natural, less tense, because of the discovery that I do not need to have an accurate understanding of God in mind before addressing him. I have been working on the idea of turning my mind and heart towards God as often as I can during the day, trying to live in a prayerful way, rather than having set times of prayer. I am also trying to listen more, and be less wordy and demanding.

I am still reeling with shock that I enjoyed my one day retreat so much, and I have begun to scheme about how to make it happen again. I could see that planning this in as a regular event would do a lot for my spiritual health. I am sorry to have made this discovery so late on – it feels as though I have missed a lot of opportunities to spend intentional time with God.

I was fully signed up to the principle of living simply before this project, if not terribly good at it in practice. I really think I have fewer and smaller piles since the declutter (Shawn might disagree) and I am determined to keep stuff flowing out of the house instead of into it. I am still working at being content and at keeping my relationships as uncomplicated as they can be.

Three Steps Forward, Two Steps Back

You might think that the discovery that God is delightful company would mean I might want to be in God's company as much as possible. You might assume that if I found the Bible interesting, edifying and transformative I would make a point of reading it frequently. You would be forgiven for assuming that I would want to do anything that not only helped me to get to know God better but which I actually found enjoyable too – but it turns out I don't. What is going on?

Busyness is perhaps part of the problem. My life, like everyone else's, is a colourful collage of competing elements. Some things get squeezed out of the picture because there is nowhere to stick them. I could reasonably use busyness as an excuse for not studying the Bible more, and perhaps I can be let off the hook for my poor record in attending prayer meetings. But deep down, I know that I am making excuses. A lot of spiritual practices can co-exist very comfortably with what I have planned in each day. I just need to do them.

The fact is, there is a mysterious resistance within me when I begin to feel I am getting deeper into my relationship with God. I can't take the heat. I lose concentration. I start messing around. I sabotage myself. If this is maddening to me, it must be enraging to God. Can you relate? I am not sure if this is a universal pattern or unique to Jo Swinney. My considered analysis of what is going on is this: I am sinful. That about sums it up. The part of me that wants to be holy is in perpetual conflict with the part of me that wants to be bad. Thankfully, the Holy Spirit is also involved in the struggle, and transformation is not my job. I have always been very reassured by these words of Paul in his letter to the Philippians: '...being confident of this, that he who began a good work in you will carry it on to completion until the day of Christ Jesus' (1:6).

The End Game

Jesus was very clear that if a person knew God their life would show it – what kind of tree you are is shown by the kind of fruit you produce. One of the most frightening warnings he gave in his Sermon on the Mount was that if we do not do the will of his Father, he will greet us in the kingdom of heaven with the words, 'I never knew you' (Matthew 7:21–23). Knowing God is going to transform us, and our transformation is not a private, inner matter. It will mean that we get involved in campaigning for the rights of the oppressed, that we go on soup runs for the homeless, that we recycle our cans, that we do everything we can to reconcile with estranged family members, that we do our taxes honestly, give money and time generously, and that we play our part in bringing about the kingdom of God on earth. A transformed life WILL result from spending time with Jesus, so don't worry about how to make it happen. Ephesians 2:10 says: 'For we are God's handiwork, created in Christ Jesus to do good works, which God prepared in advance for us to do.' It will be exciting to watch, and more so to live.

Tally Ho!

Setting myself the challenge to try out new spiritual practices and rediscover old ones has been utterly worthwhile. God hunting may be dangerous, but it is the ultimate quest any of us could go on. God wants to be hunted. He wants us to pursue him relentlessly, whatever the cost, however rough the terrain. And he will be found, because while we are hunting him, he is hunting us too.

Chapter Five: Solitude

1 Henri Nouwen, *Making All Things New*, Harper and Row, 1981, p69
2 www.personalitypage.com/ENFJ.html
3 I have written an entire book about this! It is published by Monarch, 2006, and titled *Through the Dark Woods: a young woman's journey out of depression*.
4 Bill Hybels, *Too Busy Not to Pray*, IVP, 2008, p117
5 Susan Jeffers, *Feel the Fear and Do it Anyway*, Rider & Co, 1997
6 Tricia McCary Rhodes, *Sacred Chaos*, IVP, 2008
7 Sara Maitland, *A Book of Silence*, Granta, 2008

Chapter Six: Simplicity

1 One of my professors at Regent College, Loren Wilkinson, used to make this point. We can put things in a rubbish bin and subconsciously believe that they cease to exist. The reality is that they go somewhere, probably a landfill site.
2 Gordon Macdonald talks about this distinction in *Ordering Your Private World*.
3 Fiona Castle and Jan Greenough, *Living Simply: Decluttering your Heart and Home*, Kingsway, 2006

Notes and resources

Please visit *www.scriptureunion.org.uk/ godhunting* or *www.joswinney.com* to hear the podcasts of the full interviews in each chapter.

'Come near to God…'

1 Gordon MacDonald, *Ordering Your Private World*, Thomas Nelson, 1985, p52
2 Bill Hybels, *Too Busy Not to Pray*, IVP, 2006, p35
3 Dallas Willard, *The Great Omission*, Monarch, 2006, xv

Chapter One: Prayer

1 Annie Dillard, *Pilgrim at Tinker Creek*, Harper Perennial Modern Classics, 1998
2 Jeanne Guyon, *Experiencing the Depths of Jesus Christ*, SeedSowers, 1999, p4
3 Richard Foster, *Prayer*, HarperCollins, 1992
4 Jeanne Guyon, *Experiencing the Depths of Jesus Christ*, SeedSowers, 1999, p18
5 George Buttrick, *Prayer*, Abingdon Press, 1942, p163
6 *Common Worship: Daily Prayer*, Church House Publishing, 2005
7 Brother Lawrence(author), E.M. Blaiklock (translator), *The Practice of the Presence of God*, Hodder and Stoughton, 1981, p44
8 Pete Greig, *God on Mute*, Kingsway Books, 2007

Chapter Two: Fasting

1 Jesus prefers us to fast without drawing attention to what we are doing – see Matthew 6:16–18
2 Lauren Winner, *Girl Meets God*, Authentic, 2002, p123–124
3 AC Nielson Co (www.csun.edu/science/ health/doc/tv&health.html)
4 www.cybersentinel.co.uk, quoted in The Daily Telegraph, 22nd June 2009
5 comScore via Ecoconsultancy blog, June 2007, quoted on www.barnsgraham.com
6 Gerald G. May, *Addiction and Grace*, HarperCollins, 1988, p3,4

Chapter Three: Bible

1 Nick Spencer and Graham Tomlin, *The Responsive Church: Listening to our World, Listening to God*, IVP, 2005
2 Eugene Peterson, *Eat this Book*, Hodder & Stoughton, 2006, p58
3 Craig S. Keener, *Bible Background Commentary – New Testament*, IVP, 1994
4 Gordon D. Fee, *How to read the Bible fo all its worth*, Zondervan, 1993
5 John F. Walvoord, Roy B. Zuck, *The Bible Knowledge Commentary* David C. Cook, 2002
6 Grant R. Osborne (editor), *Life application Bible Studies: Timothy and Titus*, Tyndale House, 1993.
7 Matt Redman, *The Unqu Worshipper*, Kingsway P 2001, p28

Chapter Four: Worshi

1 Brother Lawrence Blaiklock (transl *of the Presence* Stoughton, 1
2 Crux Spring Regent Co

Wor
vide
Word
on you

To try W